# OUT OF THE BLUE

# OUT OF THE BLUE

A lifetime of policing the streets.
But that was only the beginning.

## David Watson

Scratching Shed Publishing Ltd

First published by Scratching Shed Publishing Ltd in 2010
Registered in England & Wales No. 6588772.
Registered office:
47 Street Lane, Leeds, West Yorkshire. LS8 1AP

www.scratchingshedpublishing.co.uk

ISBN 978-0956252630

A catalogue record for this book is available from the British Library.

Typeset in Warnock Pro Semi Bold and Palatino

Printed and bound in the United Kingdom by
L.P.P.S.Ltd, Wellingborough, Northants, NN8 3PJ

This book is dedicated to

Andrew, Simon and Paul
- the three men who saved my life on the Isle of Skye

Dr Renshaw, Dr Templeton and Dr Shaaban
- the three men who rebuilt my broken body

Haydn
- for everything

And, of course, Julie
- sorry darling (I'll try not to do it again)

## Author's note

The vast majority of names in this book have been
changed to protect the innocent - and guilty!

# Contents

# ✳
# Preface

HAS all of this really happened in only seven weeks? How have I gone from being such a fit and strong bloke to a physical wreck in such a short period of time? My broken body is slowly starting to heal, but it bears no resemblance to how it looked the last time I saw it. My doctors say that I am lucky, but somehow I don't feel too lucky right now. I sing myself a little song, to the tune of 'Twelve days of Christmas'.

'On the eighth day of Christmas,
my true love said to me...
Eight hundred stitches (slight exaggeration)
Seven weeks in hospital
Six operations
Five broken ribs
Four femur fractures
Three broken vertebrae
Two knackered hands
One punctured lung
...And a partridge in a pear tree.'

And that isn't the full extent of my injuries. The punctured lung led to pneumonia. I have numerous broken fingers and a chunk of muscle the size of a small breakfast bowl has been torn from my left thigh. I am facing a tough battle to get back to my former self and, according to the hospital consultants, it will take me at least two years. I don't believe them; I am convinced that I will return to fitness within one year.

I HAD never intended that my little song would be heard in public. In fact, my singing voice sounds infinitely better when confined to a soundproof bathroom. And, for sure, the two-man ambulance crew who wheeled my trolley out of Ward 54 wasn't interested in what was putting a smile on my face, or what silly thoughts had been going through my head. They were just doing their job. But me, I was going home. At long last, I could begin my recovery, even if I knew I was starting from a very low point.

The outside air temperature was the first shock to my system; much cooler than I remembered it two months ago. It was autumn now and the leaves on the trees were beginning to change colour. When I had first been admitted to hospital it had been summer but the sky was now grey and overcast, sunshine a distant memory. Wheeled through the car park towards a waiting ambulance, I felt like a participant in some sort of bizarre game, trying to collect as many different modes of transport as possible. Today, an ambulance, before that a medically-equipped jet aeroplane, a helicopter air ambulance and my trusty old push bike. Quite a contrast really. And over the next few months I would be using another form of four-wheel transportation - my newly-acquired wheelchair.

It was clear that for the foreseeable future I would have

plenty of time to reminisce and reflect upon my life so far. And the irony of my spending so much of it in and around hospitals was not lost on me. Over the last twenty-six years I had spent so much time in intensive care and casualty wards that they had almost become my second home. Too many times, in my job as a policeman, I had sat with victims of violent crime or serious road traffic accidents and tried to piece together what had happened to them. On occasion, these people succumbed to their injuries and I would have the awful task of delivering the dreadful news to their loved ones. But this time it had been different. This time, *I* was the person whose body had been smashed and mutilated to the point where my nearest and dearest expected that it would be *their* loved one who would probably die.

And what about the man who caused the injuries which so very nearly ended my life? The very grand, aristocratic sounding Anton Robin Sebastian Everett? When first I saw his details on the Summons from the Sheriff Court in Scotland, I expected that he would also be the owner of some sort of title; Sir Anton Everett, Lord Anton Everett or the like. But, then again, maybe he is just an ordinary bloke like me. Other than his name, I really know very little about this man. What I do know is that he was arrested and later charged with the offence. Several months later, I was informed that he had admitted his guilt at court but, even now, I wouldn't know him if he walked past me in the street.

Before leaving the hospital I had spoken to a doctor who had been on my ward for some time. For some reason he had seemed to take a particular interest in my recovery and following our chat that morning, he smiled at me and said: 'You really should write a book. Send me a copy, I'd love to read it.' I couldn't be sure if he meant it or whether he was just being kind, but a seed was planted in my head which grew from that moment on.

## Out of the Blue

But where to start? Then, as now, I had no recollection of my first week in hospital. It is little more than a blank space, a complete void. And even in the weeks that followed, when there were numerous operations and long spells on life-support machines, my senses were suppressed with massive quantities of morphine. Yet every story has to have a beginning, a middle and an end, and mine will too, even if I can't imagine just now what that ending will be. Best, then, just to write things down and, in any case, does it really matter where it all ends up if no one will be reading it anyhow? If nothing else, putting my experience into words could be cathartic and help with my recovery.

There were physical considerations too, of course. The damage to both my hands was extensive - five of my fingers and one thumb had needed full tendon and nerve reconstruction - so the use of pens or pencils was absolutely out of the question. I wasn't capable of holding them. That left just one option - a computer keyboard, which given my limited skills as a typist at the best of times, was a prospect that hardly filled me with joy.

Then again, I never could resist a challenge.

# 1
*

# The Thrill of the Chase

I SUPPOSE it was inevitable that I would end up like this eventually. I just pushed my luck a little too far and a little too often. It started in my teenage years when I developed a love of the great outdoors. Every weekend was seen as an opportunity to go climbing, canoeing or potholing. It was a reckless and carefree existence; if I wasn't climbing a frozen waterfall without ropes then I'd be trying to rediscover the disused mineshafts or potholes in the Yorkshire Dales. My summer and winter holiday destinations would usually be within striking distance of the Swiss Alps or the Scottish Highlands.

After leaving school, my chosen career was in the building trade. In 1973, I began an apprenticeship as a carpenter and joiner and was soon to realise that a building site can be a dangerous environment. The dangers of working on scaffolding or high up on roofs are obvious and, along with my fellow apprentices, I was forever being reminded of them by my Bradford building college lecturers.

## Out of the Blue

Come 1981, Great Britain was in a deep recession and, as always happens during such times, the building trade was hit particularly hard. By this time, I had been self employed for four years and although I was making a living I was conscious of redundancies and job losses all around. Large building companies were struggling to win new contracts and that filtered down to small businesses such as mine. So when Trevor, a plumber and fine tradesman I was working in partnership with, said he'd had enough of the struggle and was ready to throw in the towel and emigrate to America to seek his fortune, it was decision time for me too.

I enjoyed being in the building trade but could see that it held few immediate prospects. Yet what other career was there? At twenty-four years old, planning to get married and having just taken out my first mortgage, I really had no idea what I wanted or would be able to do next. I envied those whose occupation gave them a guaranteed income, but I wasn't looking for white collar employment. I wanted to be outdoors, doing a job that would provide the variety of work to which I had become accustomed. When I looked at the options available I realised that they weren't good. I had never been much of a scholar. There was one possibility, however. An occupation where passing an entrance exam and fitness test were considered to be more important than formal qualifications.

I got the idea after seeing an advert which appealed to my sense of adventure in a national newspaper. I filled in my name and address and a few days later received a glossy brochure full of tempting pictures of uniformed men and women who all went about their daily work with big smiles on their faces, through the post. The brochure promised excitement, job security and the prospect of a challenging if demanding career. The hard sell worked and I now knew what I wanted to do. Within weeks I had taken a number of short exams at Bradford Central police station, which I passed with flying colours. I was going to become a police officer in what was then called the West Yorkshire Metropolitan Police. Those exams were quickly followed by a medical and interview at police headquarters in Wakefield and, by early October, I was being measured for the uniform and ready to start my new life. I had joined the boys in blue.

I wasn't unduly concerned about the potential danger of being a policeman, that was for other people to worry about. As far as I was concerned, there didn't seem to be any more risk of serious injury than might be expected working in the building trade or climbing up mountains.

I WAS one of thirty new recruits standing to attention on the drill square at Bishopgarth; that's the name of the police training facility in West Yorkshire. The booming voice of the drill Sergeant had put the fear of God in us and there was no doubting who was in charge: Sergeant Ted Baker.

Ted was a legend in his own lifetime. By now he was well into his fifties and as far as I could tell this had been his whole life's work. He had been a drill sergeant in the army before joining the police, although I never really found out if he had actually been officially promoted to sergeant or whether he was an acting-sergeant and had been given the stripes so he could be seen to have some authority over the recruits.

Not that Ted needed any visible sign of rank to impress anyone. Officers who were far more senior in rank would quake in their boots if they had the nerve to walk across his drill square when he was in full swing, screaming out his commands. He had a way of shortening some words and lengthening others so that they fit into his repertoire. We had 'eft, right, eft, right, aboowwt tern' and, finally, as his voice rose to a magnificent crescendo, the command - 'ALT!', which brought us all crashing to a full-stop. By the end of the first week we could put on a credible display.

Ted was also responsible for carrying out the inspection of recruits on the drill square. Like most of the others, I had been subject to a severe haircut two days earlier. It was almost down to the wood and this was in 1981, when many young men grew their hair onto their collar and over their ears. Ted went down the line and told us all to go to the canteen that evening, where we had the privilege of paying a barber to cut our hair once again. He then paired us all off, matching those who had been in uniformed occupations previously, such as former police cadets or ex-military, with people who were coming into this way of life for the very first time. In other words, people just like myself.

A lad called Gerry Corrodale had the misfortune to be lumbered with that responsibility in my case. That night, as we sat in his bedroom, he showed me how to bull my brand new leather boots. Gerry had been a cadet for the previous two years, so he knew what Ted expected. He showed me how to apply the polish and rub it round in circles with a soft cloth, and then how to spit on the polish and continue making the circles with the cloth. Layer upon layer of polish was built up in this way until the boots shone like glass. Or at least the left boot did, the one that Gerry had been bulling. The right boot, which was my pathetic attempt, had a much duller appearance. An hour later and he was getting bored. 'That's okay,' he said. 'We will see what he thinks of them in the morning'. I wasn't quite so confident. The difference between the boots was easily seen, but Gerry was in charge.

The following morning I ended up on the front rank, the last place that I wanted to be with what looked like an odd pair of boots. Ted barked at all the recruits to come to attention so that he could start his inspection. He began with the officers to my left, spending only a few seconds on each person. Already, though, he had found fault. One man had failed to tie his boot laces properly. Ted looked down at the laces, put his face inches from that of the young man to whom they belonged and bellowed: 'Your laces are hanging down like an old man's piles! Get them fastened properly'. Oh yes, it was funny. It always is when it's at someone else's expense. But it didn't bode well for me.

I didn't have long to wait. When my turn came, Ted first stared at my helmet. It had been carefully brushed to get rid of any trace dust or fluff and sat squarely on my head. My face was scrubbed and shaved, my hair re-cut and my tunic and trousers immaculately pressed and brushed. He seemed satisfied and hadn't even looked at my boots. Had I got away with it? it certainly seemed so when he took a step towards the next man but then, just as I was about to breathe a little sigh of relief, he stopped and suddenly looked back over his shoulder, directly at my feet. Swivelling to face me, mouth not three inches away from my own, he bellowed: 'You've got one boot shinier than the other', his warm breath nearly knocking me over backwards.

'Yes, sergeant,' was my feeble reply.

'Who showed you how to bull your boots officer?' he demanded and I had no hesitation in telling him; this was no time for misplaced loyalty. 'Corrodale,' Ted shouted at the top of his voice. Gerry took one pace forward and snapped to attention. 'This officer's boots are a disgrace. You are on nine o'clock parade tonight.' 'Yes, sergeant,' replied Gerry, no doubt cursing me inwardly.

Ted Baker was a proud man and he prepared us well for our next stage of training. This was going to be ten weeks at RAF Dishforth in North Yorkshire, where there would be recruits from all over the north east of England. But first, on the Friday, our last day with Ted, he gave us a speech which would have made the hairs on the back of my neck stand up, if I still had any. We had just finished drill practice and were much improved in only seven days. We were told to stand at ease while Ted reminded us of how, earlier that summer, riots at Toxteth, Handsworth, Brixton and other towns and cities had almost brought England to its knees. He told of how the police force had saved this country from impending disaster and said we should wear our uniforms with pride.

Upon arriving at RAF Dishforth - now in use by the police as a district training centre - the military mood continued. My car was searched and then remained outside the compound for the rest of the week. Our accommodation was in large dormitories with fourteen beds and fourteen wardrobes in each room. Two dormitories shared the basic toilet and shower facilities which were absolutely freezing, this being winter. Along with a dorm inspection every day, there was to be no exit or entry to the base between the evenings of Sunday and Friday and every time we moved from one building to the next, for meals or lessons, we were expected to march in perfect formation. In short, it was like being in prison and, worst of all, the bar was only open until 10.30pm, with lights out by 11.00pm.

As a result, it wasn't a particularly enjoyable ten weeks. Too much time was spent in the classroom studying law and there were too many exams which, in turn, led to too much pressure. We were taught self-defence and how to use our newly-issued truncheon and handcuffs. We learned first aid, life-saving techniques in the swimming pool and endured endless keep-fit sessions. I realised, though, even at that early stage, that this was not the real world. The things we were being taught in 'practical' lessons were a million miles away from what might daily be found on the streets of West Yorkshire. I couldn't wait to leave Dishforth behind.

Towards the end of our final week there, we now not-so-raw recruits were told of our postings when we returned to our respective forces. My own destination was Halifax but, within twenty-four hours, that had changed to Brighouse for operational reasons. I was beginning to see how you could be messed about but, really, at that stage the whereabouts of my posting didn't matter. All I wanted to do was get away from training school and begin some real policing.

I DIDN'T have long to wait. After two days' rest, I paraded nervously at Brighouse police station for the very first time. Of our two team-sergeants, the oldest was a friendly and laid-back sort of chap named Geoff, who had been in the police force forever and immediately tried to put me at ease. Alongside him was Frank, less welcoming and a little domineering, recently promoted and anxious to make his mark. Frank gave me a pep-talk that left me knowing precisely where I stood. 'It is our job to make sure you do your job properly,' he began. 'But we won't be with you out there on the streets, so the only way we will know how you are doing is through your paperwork.' 'Yes, Sergeant.' 'And you will only submit paperwork when you arrest or report people for offences. Remember that.' It was my first taste of good cop, bad cop.

Like new recruits everywhere I was keen to create a good impression, so I had arrived about thirty minutes early for this, my inaugural afternoon shift. That gave me plenty of time to make space in a spare wardrobe for the armfuls of uniforms and equipment I had carried in through the public entrance, this being before the days of individual lockers. Then, after meeting the sergeants, it was off to the briefing room and an introduction to the rest of the team who, on the whole, seemed like a good bunch and appeared to get on well together. I say 'on the whole' because one of the group held himself aloof, reluctant to join in with the banter and general joviality. Reluctantly, or so it seemed to me, he shook me by the hand and said his name was Steve Asquith; my tutor constable! Stood out there on the fringes, he appeared to be something of a loner, not really accepted by the rest of the team and, perhaps, not wishing to be accepted either. Hardly the best of starts I thought.

There was little time to dwell on that, however, as within the first hour I was a passenger in a Ford Escort panda car, pulling out of the car park at the back of the police station. In the driving seat was Steve, charged with keeping an eye on me and giving me a tour of the division. I couldn't decide if those tasks had been forced upon him or whether he was usually such a miserable sod but, either way, he did not seem overjoyed about the prospect of looking after me for the next four weeks.

And as for my own thoughts, well, here I was, ready to embark on a new chapter in my life as PC David Watson and feeling very uncomfortable about it. Apart from wearing an unfamiliar collar and tie, I felt terribly cramped in my new uniform, with its starched white shirt and tightly belted tunic. The handcuffs hooked on my trouser belt pressed into my back and the wooden truncheon in its special pocket down the side of my right thigh was sticking into my leg. This lot was going to take some getting used to. My right breast pocket held my pocket book and pens. In the left one was my police radio, which I was nervous about using as that would be the surest way possible of showing everyone just how new and inexperienced I actually was.

Steve, meanwhile, continued to drive around the division, pointing out the boundaries of the various foot beats and significant buildings like the Magistrates court and social security office. It was his intention to show me the town centre and then drive around the outer perimeter of our boundary to give me an overall picture. So far, so straightforward. But then, suddenly, the radio burst into life. From it came a distorted message concerning a man named Wes Barrett, who, they said, was trying to obtain goods by deception. Apparently, Barrett was in a department store on King Street and using a stolen cheque book. Steve was on the ball; he grabbed the car radio microphone and told the control room that we would attend as we were in the area.

With the car's accelerator pedal floored and our speed increased substantially, Steve tore off towards the town centre, with siren and blue flashing lights blazing. This was it - the reason I joined the police in the first place - we were on our way. Cars pulled over to let us pass and pedestrians scampered to one side, allowing us a clear road ahead. But in seconds there was a further radio message; Barrett had fled the store and was now running along Bradford Road, with a member of staff in hot pursuit. Bradford Road, now that was a stroke of luck. It was the very road we were now driving along.

'There he is,' Steve yelled, as he jumped on the brakes and the car skidded to a halt. He pointed to a man who was sprinting down the footpath towards us. Our target was on my side of the road and I got a good look at him as he ran past our car. But by the time I had opened the door he was behind us, fast disappearing into a crowd of shoppers. 'You get after him and I'll try to head him off in the car', Steve commanded.

Needing no second invitation, I jumped out of my seat and set off running, unaware that until Steve had completed a full circuit of the one-way traffic system, I was going to be on my own. Steve screeched away, accelerating hard but in the opposite direction. Soon, I was in a flat-out sprint the other way, dodging in and out of innocent bystanders while the overweight and thirty-year-old Barrett seemed quickly to be running out of steam. Eventually, I closed in; close enough to dive forward and wrap my arms around his legs, a well-timed rugby tackle which brought him crashing to earth. Laid flat on the ground, he had no fight left in him as I sat astride his back, holding him face down by the collar of his jacket. A small crowd gathered, wondering what the hell was going on. I could have done with the answer to that one myself.

Oh help, what do I do next, I thought, feeling very self-conscious. Panic began to build within me. I shook like a leaf, though whether through nerves or adrenaline - or a combination of the two - I wasn't sure. Okay, I've caught him but what do I do now? And where the hell is Steve? I knew what I was supposed to do: recite the official caution and make sure that I remembered it word-perfect. Then, give the suspect the reason for his arrest and secure the handcuffs. Unfortunately, though, I wasn't sure that I could remember the exact words of the caution and nor was I certain of the official reason for his apprehension. If nothing else, holding him there was at least allowing both of us to get our breath back. And then, with some relief, I noticed a potential saviour, a uniformed policeman by the name of PC Ray Wade walking right towards us. Earlier, Ray and I had been sat alongside each other in the police station briefing room. Never had I been so pleased to see anyone.

PC Wade strolled up and instantly assessed the situation, knowing that it was my first proper day in the job. 'As tha locked 'im up yet?' he asked, in his broad Yorkshire accent. 'Erm, no, no, not yet,' I replied. Ray looked down at the suspected villain. 'Oi, you,' he said, ensuring Barrett turned his head to face him. 'Tha's locked up fella.'

I was astounded. There was neither an official caution nor any reason given for the arrest. It was all too easy; what had I been worried about? Barrett was handcuffed where he fell and then lifted back to his feet before being bundled off to the cells in Steve's newly-arrived police car. Job done, Ray went back to his foot patrol leaving me to reflect on how this arrest had not resembled any of the 'mock' situations we had undergone at RAF Dishforth. Clearly, Ray had his own way of cautioning and arresting suspects and who was I to argue with those methods? After all, he had been a copper for nine whole months longer than me, and was already something of an old sweat.

Returning with my first prisoner, I felt like the cat who got the cream; although that joy would turn out to be short-lived. For here was an immediate introduction to the less glamorous side of police work - hour upon hour of filling in forms, taking witness statements, interviewing prisoners and searching their homes. Already I realised that the job on the streets would a damn sight more interesting - and a good deal less stressful - than the job in the police station.

# 2

## *

## Fools Rush In

NOR did it take me long to realise that the night shift was without doubt my favourite. It started at 10pm, by which time the senior officers had long since gone home - always something of a relief. This was also the point when the petty and nuisance calls stopped; no more troublesome kids or complaints about shoplifters. The dark hours were when the real criminals came out to play and I relished the opportunity of pitting my wits against them. In many ways, it was a game. They were the bad guys and I was the good guy, but we played for high stakes. If they lost, the price was a spell in prison. At least, that was how I liked to think that it would work.

One night, I was walking the beat in an old industrial area on the outskirts of Brighouse town centre and, as usual, patrolling alone. Nowadays that would be almost unheard of, but back in 1982 it was regarded as normal. On this particular evening I wandered along Birds Royd Lane and popped in to see Walter, a nightwatchman at Blakeborough

Valves, a large engineering company who operated day and night. The furnace could be seen glowing through the open doors and as I walked past I felt a blast of hot air on my face. It must have been a hot, dirty and unpleasant working environment and I did not envy the men who worked there. The heat was unbearable; no wonder the doors were wide open, even on a winter's night. Walter was an ex-policeman working as a security man to supplement his police pension. It seemed sad to me that after working shifts for thirty years in the police force, he was now back working night-shifts permanently.

After a brew and a chat with Walter, I went back to my foot patrol. It had not taken me long to learn the golden rule for any officer on the beat: make sure you find any broken windows or forced doors on your patch that have occurred during the hours of your shift. It was acceptable not to find the burglars themselves, but if the keyholder discovered that their premises had been broken into before you did, you could expect to be in trouble. So I knew what was expected of me. Identify all the vulnerable premises and give them special priority; 'vulnerable' meaning those buildings that contained anything worth stealing that could easily be sold to receivers. Such buildings were to be checked at least twice on your tour of duty, once before your meal break and once after it.

Walking back along Birds Royd Lane, I diligently checked its industrial buildings, a number belonging to small businesses. There was a builder's yard, a carpet fitter's warehouse and a couple of car repair garages. Few cars used this road in the early hours of the morning and all was quiet as I shone my torch on windows and rattled doors to make sure they were secure. Before too long it would be dawn and I was already looking forward to 05.30, when I would begin my walk back to the police station and then go home to bed.

## Out of the Blue

That was the plan anyway. For I was just about to check the last building - a small commercial garage which sold and repaired second-hand vehicles - when I noticed something was wrong. To the front of the building were several sliding concertina aluminum doors, facing onto a small forecourt. The end door was slightly ajar and damaged about halfway up. Buckled and twisted, it had obviously been crowbarred open. It hadn't been like that when I last looked, just before midnight. Suddenly, I felt tense and my heartbeat increased. Burglars were on my patch.

I knew what was expected of me, going by the book. I should stand back, keep watch on the point of entry and radio the control room to ask for back-up. But if I did that the burglars may still be inside and able to be alerted by my call. And anyway, if there were prisoners to be caught, I wanted them for myself.

So the decision was made. It was probably the wrong one but I made it anyway. I would go in alone. With my radio turned off and torch safely in my pocket, I was going to use stealth and creep in silently, using the element of surprise to arrest the intruders. Another quick survey outside revealed that the burglars hadn't even posted a look-out. Time, then, to remove my helmet - whose chrome badge would easily be seen in the faintest glimmer of moonlight. Placing it quietly on the ground, I then pulled up the collar of my greatcoat to hide my light blue police shirt.

Ready to go, I crept forward on the balls of my feet, taking care that my heels didn't touch the concrete floor and alert the burglars to my presence. So far so good. Now I had to squeeze gently through the open door, making sure that I didn't brush against it. Inside, it was dark. In fact, darker than dark. Total blackness. The only glass in the place was in three roof skylights, which the dark overcast sky rendered useless.

I stood still for a moment, allowing my eyes to adjust to

the darkness. Soon, it didn't seem quite so black and I began to recognise shapes. I could make out parked cars and where work benches were positioned. The main building consisted of four separate repair bays, each with space for one car, two of which were in use and the other two empty. I listened intently, tilting my head to the left and then to the right, in the hope of picking up the slightest sound. Nothing, though. Absolute silence everywhere except my head and my chest, where my heart beat so loudly I was sure the burglars would easily hear it. No sign of movement, either. I took a couple of paces forward to look into one of the empty bays; just a final check, then I would turn on my torch and radio the control room to contact a keyholder. I arrived too late, I thought. The burglars must have already been and gone. Nevertheless, best just to make sure of that final bay.

Suddenly, as I stepped forward into the darkness, the ground beneath me disappeared and with a sickening lurch I plummeted through a hole in the floor. Dropping like a stone, I felt a tremendous whack across the ribs and a split-second later my feet hit solid ground, legs crumpling as they crashed to earth. In a heap on my knees, I felt disoriented and struggled to catch my breath. The blow to the chest had forced the air from my lungs and left me winded; it was too late now but I scrambled frantically in my pocket for the torch.

The situation soon became clear. I had fallen around six feet into an open car inspection pit. My ribs had smashed into the metal edging along the top of the inspection pit as I made my rapid descent. The beam of the torch picked out a set of wooden steps and, once I could breathe again, I stood up and gingerly made my way up them, emerging at floor level with rather more caution than I had left it only a minute before. If any burglars had been in the garage they must surely have heard me by now, and no doubt fled while laughing their heads off.

I was angry that someone would be stupid enough to leave a car inspection pit open in the middle of the garage floor; it was a dangerous and stupid thing to do. I intended to take that up with the keyholder when he arrived. Yes, I was going to tell the proprietor of this garage exactly what I thought of him for nearly causing me a serious injury.

Better late than never, I finally radioed the control room to tell them that I had found an insecure garage and request that they should call out the keyholder. Twenty minutes later he arrived and was not in the best of moods. Dragged out of his nice warm bed at 04.00, he discovered that not only had his garage been forcibly entered, causing extensive damage to the door, the thieves had stolen the very same Mercedes that had been parked over an inspection pit. Yes, the very same inspection pit that I had just fallen down.

Clearly, it was me who had been the stupid one. The burglars had obviously broken into the garage and stolen the Mercedes before, upon leaving, attempting to close the damaged concertina door behind them. And all of it hours before I arrived on the scene, when my enthusiasm to catch the intruders in the act had clouded my better judgement. The reward for such enthusiasm? Several bruised ribs and plenty of ridicule from sympathetic colleagues.


AS with all the other raw recruits, the first two years of my police career were spent as a foot beat officer, walking an allocated area for at least seven hours in an eight-hour shift. Every police division had their own way of doing things but, at Brighouse, each new officer was allocated a specified route and was not allowed to set foot in a police car during that time. My own allocated beat was Brighouse town centre, only half a mile from the station and able to be walked in less than thirty minutes.

While patrolling this beat, I began to notice things that I hadn't before, such as how the town went through a twenty-four hour cycle, how it changed from one day to the next, and how it changed from day to night and from weekday to weekend.

The day sprang cautiously back into life at around four in the morning. It was then that the postmen could be seen driving or walking to the sorting office, often in a hurry and too busy to stop and talk. They were followed by the milkmen, who drove to the express dairy before loading their vans with that day's supply of milk. This was always my signal to stroll to the dairy myself, where I was always made welcome by a foreman who, though usually too busy for any conversation, would let me into his office to make myself a cup of tea. After walking the beat all night, it was a relief to sit down and enjoy a bit of warmth and comfort.

At about 05.30, I would head off back through the town centre, by which time the shopkeepers had begun to arrive. The greengrocers came first; unloading their fruit and veg fresh from the wholesale market in Bradford, ready for opening at eight. Next came the butchers, busily cutting up animal carcasses to display in their shop window. Then it was the turn of the dustbinmen to put in an appearance, going from shop to shop with an orange beacon flashing on the roof of their truck, abandoned in the middle of the road every fifty yards. The driver would jump in and out, leaving the cab door wide open as he went to assist his colleagues.

Most of us seldom see our towns waking up and coming to life like this, but such change is a feature of town centres and it goes on throughout the day. By nine o'clock, all the shop workers have arrived and the place is ready for an influx of customers. If the weather is fair, after a gentle trickle to begin with, the streets will be busy by ten. In the busy little West Yorkshire market town of Brighouse, the shopping continues through the day. And given the area's easy access to nearby towns and cities by bus, there are usually a fair number of retired folk around. These people are reliably friendly with a police officer walking the beat and the town's shopkeepers are also welcoming, with casual good morning chat on offer, along with a cup of tea in the storeroom at the back.

By five in the afternoon, however, you begin to notice the reverse of this cycle. Employees of the department stores simply walk out the door and set off home. Workers in the often family-owned greengrocers or butchers, on the other hand, can be seen clearing up for some time yet and then carry on working to prepare the shop for the following day. After this, a dormant period follows before the town centre switches character yet again; it is no longer a place to shop but a place to consume alcohol. As a result, it is less busy and less friendly and no longer is there a mixture of different generations and genders occupying the streets.

In fact, the population is now almost exclusively male and in the age group of eighteen to thirty. In Brighouse, there is a strong football influence and many of its young men consider themselves to be members of the Leeds United 'Service Crew'. In reality, they are just a ragtag of drunken hooligans using football as an excuse for unruly behaviour. These lads wander around the town centre pubs and share a common interest, namely Leeds United. What they seek is recognition and respect from other gangs, on account of their ability to cause fights and damage property. These gangs of males strut from pub to pub getting drunk and 'proving' their masculinity.

At weekends, pub fights are even more common and the police will only be called if the landlord is unable to eject the perpetrators himself, or with the help of his doormen. The drunks want to fight - if there are any outsiders in town then they make good opposition, otherwise the police are the target, in an environment unrecognisable from that during daylight hours. Eventually, these drunks will go home, get themselves arrested or leave for the nightclubs of Halifax, as Brighouse begins to nod off once more. The town centre policeman will soon have time on his hands again, time to walk to the taxi office and share a cup of tea with the same drivers who have just shipped all the drunkards home. Then it's back out onto the deserted streets, noseying around the back of the shops, checking doors and windows, listening for rogue alarms. In the 1980s, surveillance cameras were unheard of - most shops didn't even have a security grill over the window. The only deterrent was the sight of a uniformed officer. This was taken so seriously in Brighouse that the town centre was patrolled twenty-four hours a day, seven days a week.

Sunday morning was different. There weren't any postmen, milkmen or early-morning shopkeepers but, by 05.30, there was a different group of people on the streets. One group was the anglers, who would often stop and chat while waiting for friends to join them, before heading down to the River Calder or the canal. One Sunday morning I encountered a very jovial group, one of whom wanted to share a tale he found highly amusing. The previous weekend, he'd bumped into another policeman walking the beat. 'And do you know what his name was,' he asked, struggling to contain himself. 'No,' came the reply. 'PC... Arthur Beer. Arthur Beer! Do you get it? Arthur Beer!' And they all fell about in fits of laughter. I had known Arthur Beer for some time and, although it was rather an amusing name, I didn't find it quite as hilarious as this group did.

# 3

*

# Good Coppers Don't Get Wet

AFTER a while, I began to think of myself as part of the fabric of Brighouse, convinced that very little happened in that town centre that I wasn't aware of. I was part of the community and even now, some thirty years later, I still feel an affinity and fondness towards the place.

On the whole, though, I was no different to all the other probationary police constables. Soon, I began to think that I had been walking the beat long enough and was anxious to obtain my 'driving permit'; ie the authority to drive panda cars. But before that could happen there was a dreaded three-week police driving course to be successfully completed. Merely to take it was regarded as an achievement because you could not be trained to drive police cars until you were thought competent enough to work independently. Being a police driver, therefore, almost felt like promotion. You no longer walked the beat every day and were regarded as one of the more trusted and senior officers on the team.

Happily, for me, the course proved no problem and a few

weeks after achieving the distinction I was on mobile patrol during a night shift in Brighouse. The weather was foul - rain came down in stair rods - the sort of night when you really appreciated being in a patrol car rather than on foot. Even the windscreen wipers were struggling to cope. Inside, I was nice and dry, the heater was blasting out warm air and all was well with the world. Or at least it was until a car came hurtling past, driven by a lunatic who thought he was a stunt driver.

I could hardly ignore driving like that, even if I didn't relish the thought of getting out of my nice warm car to go and speak to him. If I didn't stop and have a word with this idiot, he might kill himself - or, worse, someone else. And it would at least give me the chance to put my newly-acquired driver training skills to the test. The vehicle in question was an old style Ford Escort, one of the easiest cars to steal. Just about any car key would open the doors, then a screwdriver to turn on the ignition and you're away. Maybe it's stolen, I thought, or maybe it's just a boy racer - either way, I'd better check it out. I began to follow the car and even though there was nothing else on the road,was struggling just to catch up. But after another half-mile of determined driving, I was right behind him.

He must have seen me getting closer in his rear view mirror but, still, would not slow down. Time to put into practice those freshly-acquired techniques. Illuminating the blue rotating roof light and flashing my headlights was a clear signal for him to stop. Yet he didn't even slow down. Instead, the driver increased his speed and started to pull away. Was this really going to be my first car chase?

On the radio to the control room, I gave the registration number of the vehicle that was, by now, being driven very dangerously indeed around the streets of Brighouse, its driver showing no intention to stop. My earlier assumptions proved correct; the car had indeed been stolen that same evening and, yes, this was now my first official police pursuit. I stayed as close to my quarry as I could while his driving became even more erratic, taking blind bends on the wrong side of the road and speeding through red lights. The rain, meanwhile, continued to pour, with water from the puddles at the side of the road splashing high onto the walls of buildings as he sped on by, trying to get me off his tail, his obvious desperation matched only by my determination to arrest him for theft of the car. All the while, I kept up a continuous commentary on the radio in the hope that another police car, driven by my colleague Phil Mead, would come to my assistance and maybe block the road ahead.

Hard as I tried, I was unable to make any impression whatsoever on the stolen car, its driver kept well ahead of me without any real difficulty. Maybe he had more to lose and was prepared to take more risks than I was. After all, the last thing I needed was to crash a panda when I had only just got my permit to drive. Despite my efforts on the radio there was still no sign of Phil and he was driving the only other police car in our division.

Then, just as I was beginning to give up any hope of making my first car chase arrest, the driver of the stolen Escort hit a mini-lake covering the entire width of the road. The car aqua-planed across the vast puddle just as its driver was approaching a right-hand turn. Out of control and careering to the other side of the road, the Escort's wheels locked up; it wasn't going to make the bend. Instead, the driver collided head-on with the boundary wall of Rastrick Golf Club while I bellowed into the radio: 'He's crashed, he's crashed...he's out and running.' Rammed into the stone wall almost as far as the windscreen, this particular car would be going nowhere without a recovery vehicle.

Result! But what about the renegade driver himself? He had no intention of giving himself up yet; having climbed out of the wrecked car, he quickly jumped over the wall and into the grounds of the golf course. He was a quick and agile youth as he scampered over the half-demolished wall, but now I was really confident that I would catch him. At the time I was a far better runner than a driver and there was no way I would lose him in a foot chase, despite the continued torrential rainfall.

Snatching the car keys from the ignition, I was out of the car and after him without pausing to pick up my coat or torch from the glove compartment. Once over the wall, I was into a small wooded area and, within seconds, soaked to the skin. Each time I brushed against a tree, the raindrops on its leaves were disturbed, giving me a fully-clothed shower. The trees also blocked out any moonlight and it was so dark that I couldn't see my hand in front of my face. It had been a serious error to leave the torch behind, and an even bigger mistake to leave my coat.

The sound of movement came from out ahead, someone running and breaking the small branches underfoot, and I continued to give chase, running blindly in what was, I hoped, the right direction. In less than two minutes I had lost sight of the lad completely, but was still following the noise of someone crashing through the undergrowth. Before too long, I began to head downhill on a steep and slippery bank. On more than one occasion I ended up on my backside, the rainwater now soaking through trousers and underwear as I landed on the wet earth. The darkness made it impossible to see what lay at the bottom of the incline - I was running into the unknown.

At which point came a muffled shout, as someone cried out in pain ahead. That's good, I thought, he must have run into something. With a bit of luck he will have hurt himself and be forced to slow down, thereby increasing my chance of apprehending him. This was all the encouragement I needed and I increased my pace. Sprinting now, I blindly charged forward into the gloom, with my arms raised before me as protection from the twigs and branches scratching at my face and arms. Gravity was on my side, too - or so I thought - pushing me down the steep slope faster and faster until I came to a sudden and unexpected halt.

My legs had crashed into an unseen, low stone wall at the bottom of the banking. It was only about knee-high but that was high enough! As my legs stopped dead, the momentum of my upper body threw me forward and I flew through the air. My hands hit the ground first as I landed in a puddle on the wet and slippery grass, before skidding forward like a punctured hovercraft on my forearms and chest. Completely soaked from head to foot - it would have been impossible to be any wetter - I looked up and saw that I was on one of the golf course greens. At least now I knew what had caused my car thief to yelp out in pain. He had obviously fallen over the same wall a few moments earlier.

Thoroughly winded, I looked around and spotted the desperado running off into the distance, only now with a noticeable limp, I was relieved to note. So, struggling to my feet, I set off after him again, gradually increasing my speed from a fast walk to a slow run. In fact, given that I too was by now limping, a slow hobble would be more accurate, as I continued to give my radio audience back in the station an out-of-breath commentary. To be honest, I could have done with some help but, still, there was no sign of Phil Mead. Where on earth had he got to? Probably sat somewhere warm and dry, looking out of a window at the rain and feeling rather pleased with himself, I reflected. Yet although I still did not have the energy to sprint, I had continued to gain doggedly on the thief.

By now, the lad in question was running out of steam. But once again he sought an escape route, this time via the stone boundary wall that separated the golf course from the main road beyond. At this point, the wall was about ten-feet high but, because the road was elevated, it was only around three-feet tall on the other side. More handily, it also sloped back at a nice gentle angle towards the golf course, making it easy to climb. As a last-ditch escape route, it wasn't bad, but I was determined not to give up; this character was going to be my prisoner and I would make sure he was charged with every offence I could think of. His arrest was going to make all my pain and effort worthwhile.

Another factor in the escapee's favour was that this particular wall was of the dry stone variety with no mortar between individual stones and plenty of holds for the hands and feet. I tried to sprint the last few yards, lungs bursting and legs like jelly, but he had nearly reached the top just as I arrived at the bottom. I could still catch him. All I had to do was reach up with an outstretched arm and grab his foot and he would be mine. I reached up, ready to do just that when there, through the rain, a familiar face looked down on me, stopping me in my tracks and rooting me to the spot.

Standing next to the main road, looking over the wall, was Phil Mead my, until now, absent colleague. From a comfortable distance, he had watched the whole scene unfold on the golf course below. Casually reaching over and grabbing the errant youth by the hair, I heard him say: 'You're under arrest, pal, on suspicion of stealing a car.' Too exhausted to climb, I stood at the bottom looking up while Phil handcuffed the culprit, not for my benefit but for his own. Job done, he then leaned back over the wall, gave me a quick smile and a cheery wave, and drove off in his police car with MY prisoner in tow.

I could not believe what I had just seen and heard. I had chased this youth for miles in a dangerous car chase. I had pursued him through woodland in the dark, my face and arms covered in scratches, before hitting and then diving, head first over a stone wall, bruising and grazing my shins. Blood was seeping down my legs and soaking into my socks. My torn and filthy uniform was so wet I looked as if I'd been for a swim in the River Calder. I felt shattered. And not only, at the end of all that, had Phil stolen my prisoner, to add insult to injury he had also abandoned me on the golf course without so much as offering a lift back to my car. They say there is no honour among thieves. Nor is there much among policemen.

The thirty minutes it took to walk back to my car gave me plenty of time to feel sorry for myself. I hobbled back up the hill and it continued to rain, but that no longer seemed to matter. I climbed into the car with the wet trousers and shirt sticking to my skin, and now the seat would get soaked too. Driving back to the station to change into some dry uniform, I wondered if I would get thanks or recognition for my efforts, not to mention my tired and battered legs? More likely, I would be told off by the sergeant for being so scruffy.


ONE of a police officer's most unpleasant tasks is to deliver bad news, particularly with regard to a death in the family. You never know what sort of reaction to expect. Sometimes there will be dumb acceptance, with relatives in an almost trance-like state. On other occasions, people will fall to the floor and wail continuously. And there is a third reaction that can be most unexpected. I have actually seen joy and relief on the faces of the next of kin, perhaps as a result of the deceased having been engaged in a long and painful battle against cancer, and now at peace and no longer in pain. Until you knock on that door you have no way of knowing.

In the early hours of one particular morning, I was required to deliver a message such as this to a house next to a railway line at Hipperholme, near Halifax. On account of its position, the residence in question did not have vehicular access, so I had to leave the police car half a mile away and approach it via a ten-minute walk at the side of the railway tracks. The weather was atrocious. It was raining heavily with a strong horizontal wind and, as I trudged along with my head down and coat collar pulled up, it wasn't long before I was soaked right through. Eventually, though, I made out the solitary building ahead, clearly a one-time railway signalman's house and untouched in over a century by the look of it. The isolated little building was dark and spooky but I would have gladly gone inside if only to escape the horrible conditions. As usual, however, I had no idea of what to expect by way of reaction, since my visit related to an old lady who had died in a nursing home. Apparently, she had lived here with an elderly brother. He might be traumatised or expecting the news but, as everyone knows, a policeman knocking at your door at three o'clock in the morning usually signals the worst.

I knocked loudly on the door and waited a minute or two but there was no reply. Perhaps he had already been told of his sister's death and was at the nursing home right now. I knocked again, louder this time, cursing the fact that I was now really wet and shivering. Still there was no reply. I was just about to give up and begin the long walk back to the car when a light was switched on in a small upstairs window. At least I now knew that someone was home.

Looking up, I saw an old man's face staring back at me. I waved and expected that he would come downstairs and let me in. Instead he remained exactly where he was and then began banging on the window frame to try and prise it open, quite a feat since it obviously hadn't been opened in years. By now, I had composed myself and knew what I was about to say, while hoping that I wouldn't have to conduct the conversation like this. If invited inside I would be much happier (and drier) and more able to confirm the old man's identity, ensuring that I was at the right house. Once that was done, I could then pass on my message about his sister as sensitively as possible. The old man had other ideas. After several thumps of his fist the window eventually gave and he shouted: 'What do you want?'

'Hello, Mr Greenacre,' I replied. 'It's the police. I've come about your sister, Alice. Could you let me in so that we can have a private word please?'

For a moment there was no response, while he pondered my request. I looked up, using my hand to shield my eyes from the torrential rain; he stood in dumb silence, looking down at the half-drowned figure below. In his grubby string vest, set off by a large beer belly, he cut quite a picture. I daren't even consider what he was wearing on the bottom half. Come on you silly old bugger, I'm getting drenched here, I thought. But of course that would have been far too easy. He seemed determined to remain where he was and leaned forward, before yelling: 'Is she dead?'

Is she dead? What sort of question is that to ask of a police officer standing in torrential rain in the middle of the night? To say I was taken aback is an understatement. In fact I was gobsmacked and couldn't think of anything other to say than: 'Well, yes. I'm sorry to tell you, she *is* dead.'

At which, with no further ado, he slammed the window shut and disappeared back into the bedroom. Our chat, it seemed, was over. In less than a minute, the bedroom light was turned off and away I went into the wind and rain while he climbed back into his nice warm bed. As I walked back to the car with rainwater now seeping down the inside of my shirt and trousers, I reflected on Mr Greenacre's response. Maybe he had been expecting his sister's demise for some time or maybe he was just glad to have rid of her, I didn't know. One thing is certain, I never passed on another death warning under such circumstances.

# 4

\*

# Streetwise at Last

PC John Walker had an appearance that would frighten small children. He stood over six feet tall with a solid build and a heavy square jaw. Most notably, he did not appear to possess a neck; his head sat squarely on his shoulders, the result of an incident from his days in the Royal Navy when, after spending the night with a lady in her flat, her husband returned home unexpectedly. In his desperation to escape undetected, John jumped from her balcony and suffered serious injury. His subsequent physical stature disguised a wicked sense of humour he was often unable to control.

As for myself, by 1985 I had been trained as a Tutor Constable, with a mission to introduce new recruits to the practical ways of policing the streets. I would go on to fill this role over several years but, back then, John was my latest 'probationer'. After a few weeks I was satisfied that he was ready to start taking the lead role in simple tasks, such as taking details of crime reports from members of the public.

## Out of the Blue

One evening, we were sent to an address in the Shelf area of Halifax. Nothing too complicated, we were going to take a report of a burglary. Food had apparently been stolen from a freezer in a garage at the side of a very grand house. John said that he wanted this to be his first ever crime report and assured me he knew which questions to ask and the information required. My role, therefore, was to remain silent and only become involved if John missed something vital to the completion of the crime report.

Although John was very inexperienced as a policeman, this was disguised to a certain extent by his more mature years. He looked like a knowledgeable officer and I was impressed with how he obtained the personal details of the clearly wealthy householder. She was an upper-middle class lady with a posh accent who spoke down to us in a rather condescending way. Having gone through the formalities, she showed us into a garage that was as big as most people's house, where the freezer was located. Along with the freezer, there was a washing and drying machine and various other appliances. John continued to ask all the right questions: 'Exactly what has been stolen?', 'What is the value of the missing food?' etc, and all was going well until he asked her when she suspected the crime had taken place.

The lady had difficulty answering this; she couldn't remember when the garage had last been checked and was unsure over a period of the last few days. In searching for inspiration, she looked up to the ceiling and put her index finger to her lips, wracking her brain for the answer. After a while she said: 'Well, I didn't come in here on Sunday and I know that for certain because, on that afternoon, we'd had a guest for dinner.' I saw nothing in this innocent remark. It seemed a perfectly reasonable thing to say but John saw things differently. He just couldn't resist the opportunity and, without drawing breath, replied: 'Oh....did you really?

We prefer chicken.' At which, I almost collapsed laughing and was unable to stop my shoulders bobbing up and down. I had to turn my back on John and the Lady of the Manor and pretend that I was examining the door that had been forced open by the thieves. John, on the other hand, didn't show the slightest flicker of a smile. Thankfully, the lady either didn't hear the remark or, diplomatically, deliberately chose to ignore it. Somehow we left the house without any further embarrassment.

As we returned to the car, John and I howled at the mental picture he had conjured up; a guest laid on the dining table, trussed up like a Christmas turkey, half a clementine shoved into their mouth, eyes bulging in sheer terror. 'Henry, will you carve today?' 'Of course, darling. Would you like breast or leg? I would quite like the liver myself.' We kept up that silly repartee all the way back to Brighouse.


WE all get frightened sometimes, some of us more easily and more often than others. As a policeman, by and large, you learn to control your fears but, on one occasion, I was almost too scared to speak. Even then it was in a shaky and quivering voice, into my police radio.

'Foxtrot Bravo One to control,' I said. 'I'm sure I've just seen a bloke levelling a shotgun at me, as I drove around Thornton Square.'

The reply was short and direct, with not a single word wasted. 'Control to Foxtrot Bravo One. Your message is understood. We'll get you some back-up straight away.'

It didn't seem right. This was Brighouse, West Yorkshire. Not Toxteth or Moss Side or even Brixton. Gun crime was practically unheard of. But what to do now? This was the mid-1980s. Back-up would be just another unarmed officer in a panda car, not the full-scale firearms operations of a decade later. The time was around four in the morning and the town centre was deserted; no one within half a mile. And thanks to the one-way system, there wasn't even any passing traffic.

I had been cruising along Bethel Street, no faster than walking pace really, before eventually coming into Thornton Square, which isn't square at all; in fact it's round, rather like a roundabout with a raised flowerbed. Here the road turns through ninety degrees to the right and goes along the side of Wellington Arcade, a modern shopping centre containing around fifteen shops with a covered precinct running right through its middle. The precinct starts at Park Street and comes out at Commercial Street. Both entrances had been out of view when I saw what I thought was the gunman.

I had to go around again, to get another look. I continued driving, crawling along at three miles per hour, maybe even slower, following the one-way route around the perimeter of Wellington Arcade, back into Commercial Street and then right into Park Street. Not surprisingly at that time of day, it was very quiet. The town was deserted. Had my eyes been playing tricks on me? I was tired - could I trust them? Then it was back into Thornton Square and still no sign of the gunman, as my doubts increased. I HAD seen him, I was sure. A man in dark clothing with his back to the wall, holding a shotgun - or air rifle - pulled tight into his right shoulder with the barrel pointed straight at me. Only a glimpse, no more than that; a split second and then he was gone and out of sight. The situation was very threatening.

Of course, I could just have carried on driving, out of the town centre and safely off into the suburbs. I could have ignored the matter or kept quiet about it, after all I wasn't one hundred per cent sure of what I'd seen and no one need ever know. Perhaps that is what I should have done. That is certainly what my wife and children would have wanted me to do. It's probably what I would have advised anyone else to do, but the thought never even occurred. No matter how frightened I was, my conscience simply wouldn't allow me to hide or run away. It may have been that speech made by my former drill sergeant, Ted Baker, when he spoke of how the police had brought this country back from the brink of disaster during the inner-city riots. For sure, it had made an impression on me that lasted throughout my police career.

But now I was a married man with kids. Was I needlessly putting myself in danger? And for what? There was no one else in the area other than me and the gunman. I couldn't even claim that I was protecting the public because there weren't any members of the public anywhere. Two or three minutes had passed since my radio message, enough time to drive slowly around the arcade once again. I heard from the control room that my back-up would be Jim Dent, the only other patrol car driver in the division.

The elusive gunman had to be somewhere, but where? I circled around once more, slowly, very slowly, with the car window wound down, the better to pick up the slightest sound. And then suddenly, after turning into a still-deserted Commercial Street, there he was at the entrance of the precinct, standing perfectly still and looking straight at me.

I stopped the car not ten paces from where he stood, clad in green combat jacket, black jeans and boots. Was that a mistake? Should I have sped past and radioed that I had located the target? It was difficult to read anything from his facial expression because a thick black beard obscured much of it. And while at first I couldn't take my eyes off the gun, now pointing down at the ground and less threatening, my heart was still racing. Then it came to me. I recognised him.

'Brian! It's Brian Conway isn't it? Are you alright?'

He didn't reply. He just carried on staring. My voice was

steady now. I was trying to sound friendly and supportive. I had arrested this man a few months earlier for drunkenness but we hadn't fallen out, and I was glad about that now.

'Brian, what's the gun for?'

I remained in my car, but still he didn't reply. He seemed far away, distant, his eyes were wide open but not really seeing. I wasn't even sure he could hear what I was saying, maybe he was on drugs, but I couldn't tell from here. I opened the car door tentatively, talking in a soft and gentle voice. He was no longer menacing, as long as that shotgun stayed pointing at the ground I felt safe, well, fairly safe anyway. I moved five yards closer. 'Brian, will you give me the gun then we can get this thing sorted out?' Silence again. He began to edge backwards, very deliberately, into the precinct, glaring at me intently and breathing in a sinister way, clearly the victim of some sort of mental disorder. Each time I stepped forward, he stepped back. There was no plan on my part, I was just hoping for the best.

'Brian, you remember me, don't you? We were alright last time, why don't you just give me the gun and then we can talk about it?'

Again, he didn't answer as he mirrored every step I took. Soon, we had travelled half the length of the precinct. Our pace was slow, painfully so. I hoped it was slow enough to allow Jim to arrive but I still had no idea how it would end. Then, thankfully, there Jim was, standing behind Brian. I hadn't heard his car pull up and there hadn't been any messages on the radio, so he must have used the entrance from Park Street. Either way, Brian hadn't seen him yet. Jim approached Brian from behind at the same steady pace as I was approaching from the front. I kept talking to Brian; at least the sound of my voice might hide any sound that Jim may make. I prayed that Jim had turned his radio off, we wouldn't want Brian to panic. But now what? Should we rush him before he had time to aim the shotgun? Was it worth the risk? And, if not, what were the alternatives? So many questions, so little time.

Then, Brian heard footsteps. A quick glance over his right shoulder confirmed Jim's presence. Trapped, would Brian take fright and use the gun? All three of us stopped instantly in our tracks. Too tense to talk now, I didn't trust my own voice, but somehow blurted out: 'Brian, give us the gun.' Slowly and to my great relief he did just that, raising the gun in his right hand and extending his arm above his head, allowing Jim to lift it gently but firmly from his hand. With the drama over and my head pounding from the tension, Brian was arrested and taken to the police station, where he would also get to see a doctor.

There was no need for handcuffs, he rode back to the station in the front passenger seat, silent, docile and compliant. And, as it later turned out, the shotgun had not in fact been loaded. Despite my initial fear, I had never really been in any danger. 'Why did you do it Brian?'I asked. 'Why were you walking around town with a shotgun in the middle of the night?' But he didn't answer, not a single word. I made him a cup of tea but, by six in the morning at the end of my shift, Brian was still in the cell waiting for the doctor to make an assessment of his mental health.

The following evening, I enquired about Brian and was told he had been sectioned under the Mental Health Act. Apparently, he had fallen out with his girlfriend, taken lots of drugs and then gone walking with the gun because he wanted to be arrested. Police tactics were changing rapidly during the 1980s. If Brian had acted this way ten years later, there is little doubt he would have been shot by a firearms team.

# 5

## *

# One Extreme to the Other

SATURDAY night, 1987. Myself and two inexperienced officers are in a police van on public order patrol outside a ground floor council flat in Elland town centre, not an area I am too familiar with. The radio message sounds serious, a report of a stabbing. The message goes on to say that an ambulance is en route. We arrived within minutes of the call but there is no obvious sign of what has just taken place inside.

I park the van up and we walk towards the door - it has been left wide open. Inside the flat, all is dark and a corridor leads from the exterior towards a number of internal doors giving access to various rooms. As we walk in, I shout that we are the police. All is quiet and I wonder if the message was a hoax. Then comes the sound of quiet sobbing from a room at the end of the corridor, the living room it turns out.

The person doing the sobbing is a woman, sitting on a tall stool in a corner of the room. She has her back to us and doesn't look up as we walk in. Her feet rest on a rail running between the legs of the stool. Her legs are trembling so much her feet keep slipping off. She is crying uncontrollably and her whole body is shaking. Her face is hidden by her arms, which rest on a sideboard. My first impression is that she is about thirty years old, quite tall and slim, but her face remains a mystery. She is clearly very distressed and so emotional that she is unable to speak; there is just the continual sound of sobs and frequent sniffing of her nose.

Something serious has happened but we don't yet know what. The room is poorly lit by only a single table lamp. I look around in the half-light and spot a man on the floor, on his back and motionless. Moving towards him, I can see no clear sign of injury, there are no obvious stab wounds visible but he has to be the person referred to in our radio message. The officers with me are John Gill and Nick Hall, both of whom I know can be relied upon despite their inexperience. John and I approach the unconscious male, who doesn't appear to be breathing. There are no signs of life but, at the same time, I am convinced that he can't possibly be dead. He doesn't look how a dead person should.

By then, dead bodies are nothing new to me. I have seen dozens of them, whether in their home after having died of natural causes or on the road in horrific car crashes, but never anything like this. I am almost overwhelmed by a feeling of panic. I am trained in basic first aid but this is way beyond that and not something that a policeman expects to deal with.

Silently, I reminded myself of the priorities; it's got to be CPR, that's right, thirty quick compressions of his chest. Place one hand on top of the other and press with the heels of the hands. Then two emergency breaths before repeating the process until he starts breathing. First, check the airway, making sure that there is no obstruction in his throat. Tilt his head back. Right, that's done. Let's get started.

John knelt down at one side of the casualty, opposite me.

We had a few whispered words, both reassuring the other that we were about to do it correctly. I began the chest compressions, counting out loud, one to thirty. Then I leaned back as John held open the casualty's mouth. He leaned over him and gave two long deep breaths. The chest briefly inflated slightly but then subsided and remained still.

We tried again. And again. And again. Still no change. We swopped roles, John doing the chest compressions and me the emergency breaths. It was a strange sensation when I covered the mouth of another man with my own, almost an assault on my senses. I felt his course skin and growth of stubble, there was also the strong smell of beer, but most unnerving was the touch of human flesh that felt completely lifeless.

This wasn't going according to script. The casualty is supposed to cough once, maybe twice, and then begin to breath by himself, but this wasn't working. I watched for the tell-tale signs of a rising and falling chest but it was hopeless. There was no movement. Nick began speaking to the female and we could hear the broken conversation. Between sobs, the woman said that she'd stabbed him, her husband, once in the chest. She pointed to a bread knife on the sideboard before her. Nick brought it over to show us. It was twelve inches in length and came to a very sharp point. It didn't take much imagination to guess what sort of damage such a knife could do to a person. Even in the subdued light of this room, we could see that the leading four or five inches of the blade were smeared with wet blood.

Up to now we hadn't even seen any injury. With a rising sense of urgency we tried to find the stab wound, not really knowing what to do if we found it. I lifted up his shirt and saw a horizontal mark, it was only about one inch long but directly in line with his heart. The blade had passed between two of his ribs and didn't look serious enough to claim a man's life. There was a complete absence of blood which made me think that perhaps it may not be so serious after all. For some reason I had convinced myself that a lack of blood meant that he couldn't really be dying.

Many minutes had passed since we first entered that room and there was still just the three of us there, John, Nick and I, together with the woman and her dying husband. I desperately wanted the ambulance crew to attend so that I could hand over responsibility to them. Nick took over for a couple of minutes and I stepped outside to radio the control room and ask what was happening. All they could confirm was that the ambulance had been called and was on its way. I felt a tremendous weight of responsibility for this man and knew that John and Nick would expect me to know what to do, but on this occasion they were wrong. I had never been in a situation like this before either.

I went back inside, the casualty wasn't responding to our amateurish attempts to revive him, then a horrible gurgling noise began to emerge from his throat. Somewhere in the dim and distant past I'd heard that this is often referred to as the death rattle, the last sound a dying person makes before passing away. I had to do something; anything. I put my arms under the man's head and shoulders and lifted him up into a sitting position. Maybe this movement would clear his throat and allow him to start breathing, relieving me of this tremendous burden, the weight of responsibility smothered me.

As we sat him up, the gurgling stopped but the knife wound on his chest visibly opened and bled for the first time. A continuous trickle of blood seeped from his chest to his stomach, before collecting around his leather belt. This wasn't working and we may even have made it worse, so we quickly laid him back down again. I was at a complete loss.

We didn't know what else to do other than continue mouth to mouth and cardiac massage, but I knew in my own mind that he was either dying or already dead. His wife hadn't moved, she remained on the stool, a mess of dignified but uncontrollable sobbing.

Time passed slowly and it felt like an eternity before the ambulance crew arrived. When they did, I was relieved to see they had a police sergeant in tow. I walked over to them and spoke in a hushed voice because I didn't want the woman to hear what I was about to say. In a whisper, I said that, in my opinion, the casualty had already died. The sergeant looked aghast so I repeated myself, this time a little louder. 'What?' he said. 'Did you say he's dead?' I nodded my head to confirm this and silently mouthed the words again. 'Oh, fucking hell,' he blurted, but what happened next was astounding. I had tried with great difficulty to hold my own emotions together but, upon handing over responsibility, the two ambulance men and our sergeant flew into an instant state of panic. They dashed straight back out of the flat and into the street.

There was nothing else to do but return to the victim and, along with John and Nick, continue the futile effort to bring him back to life. If his wife hadn't been present, we might well have given up some time ago. It was tough to accept but this man was a lost cause. Outside, the unqualified ambulance crew called for more experienced paramedics, while the sergeant showed even less sign of wanting to take control of the situation. He radioed CID.

Eventually, the ambulancemen came back, but it was too late. There was no sign of life and there never was going to be. The man's body was covered with a green blanket - there was no point moving him now. This was a crime scene and, as such, it was important that nothing was disturbed before an investigation took place.

Soon, the flat was being overrun with CID, and they were followed by police photographers and scene of crime officers. The woman was arrested and the body of her husband taken away to the mortuary. Outside a crowd had gathered and I tried to obtain the details of any potential witnesses. I spoke to a lady who was a friend of the arrested woman who said that she had been out with her earlier that evening and visited a pub in Elland town centre. While there, they saw the woman's husband, who was drunk. This lady knew from previous experience what that meant: he would come home and beat his wife. To try and prevent this, the suspect had returned home and lain in wait with the breadknife.

Suddenly I felt surplus to requirements. Thirty minutes ago we were this man's only hope, now we were in the way. We were told to leave the crime scene and resume patrol, making sure that we provided written statements before going off duty.

It turned out that this couple had a history of domestic violence and, when she entered a guilty plea to a charge of manslaughter, the courts looked upon the woman's case sympathetically. She was sentenced to two years in prison, suspended for two years. The Judge passed comment that this woman's children had already lost their father and, if he had passed a custodial sentence, they would also lose their mother.

'YOU just don't get the characters in this job anymore'. A comment usually made by middle-aged policemen bemoaning the loss of older peers. There was however one man who fit that description perfectly. This particular character's name was Harry Buttersby and he was my inspector at Brighouse for a couple of years in the mid-1980s.

## Out of the Blue

Known throughout the division as 'Mad Harry', he was a stickler for tradition and didn't go along with change just for the sake of it. He wanted the daily briefing to be carried out in the traditional way, which meant that as he entered the briefing room everyone was called to stand to attention. Officers were expected to be in full uniform with helmet in place. If the briefing preceded a night-shift, it was expected that officers would produce their 'appointments', i.e. your truncheon, handcuffs and torch. These items were inspected by Harry, who walked up and down the ranks pointing out any apparent failings, such as overlong hair, any sign of stubble or the absence of equipment.

By this time I had been a police officer for three or four years and this was not something previously encountered. Before Harry arrived on our team, briefings had been much more informal. We would often remain seated throughout and even have a cup of tea with the inspector and shift sergeant. The briefing items would then be read out and discussed in a conversational manner, there wouldn't be any formal parade. It was the modern way of doing things and fairly widespread throughout the force at that time. But that wasn't the way Harry did it. It made his day if he found fault and there was seldom a day when he didn't, although it was always done in a fairly light-hearted manner.

After a few months, it became obvious that Harry's bark was worse than his bite so, during one of these briefings, we decided to test his sense of humour. It was the start of a night-shift and all the PCs entered the briefing room. There were ten of us in total and we sat in two rows facing the lectern from where Harry would deliver his briefing. Each of us adjusted our uniform in a way that would give Harry a reason to criticise our appearance. One man had his helmet on at a jaunty angle, another had his trouser leg tucked into a sock. Someone else's tunic buttons were misaligned, while

I removed my clip-on tie and placed it in my pocket. Harry would not be amused.

The duty sergeant was next to enter the room. He looked us up and down and a broad smile broke out across his face. Shaking his head, he said: 'He's going to go mad and I mean really mad. I hope you lot know what you're doing'. We had been warned but were prepared to take the risk. And then came Harry; he could be heard marching up the staircase. As he entered the briefing room the sergeant shouted 'stand up, please,' the signal to come to attention. In marched Harry, his appearance, as always, immaculate. He wore full uniform with his cap placed neatly upon his head. Marching along the front row of officers he could not fail to notice trousers tucked into socks, misaligned buttons and all the other forms of improper dress.

The duty sergeant pretended he hadn't noticed anything amiss and stayed silent. Harry's face twitched as he walked past, clocking each and every item. I struggled to stifle a smirk as he looked directly at my neck and missing tie. He passed no comment, turned around and marched along the rear row, again without comment. Upon passing the last man he swivelled and marched promptly out, bellowing at the sergeant that he would not take today's briefing because his men were 'taking the piss'. When he was safely out of earshot we all fell about, including the sergeant. But Harry was to have his way and, the following day, we were back to the formal and traditional approach.

THE police force was becoming more modernised but 'Mad Harry' resisted in his usual way. His briefings were a continual source of amusement, an insight into a bygone era. However, these were still the days of paper reports rather than computer generated items. The normal procedure was that the inspector would stand at the front and read out reports of crimes, forthcoming events or wanted persons. The paper reports would then be placed back on the lectern to be read out to the next shift.

One day Harry was reading out the various items when he got to one particular bit that caused him to pause. He slowly re-read it to himself while we waited for him to enlighten us as to what it was all about. It was obvious from his demeanour that something was amiss. His face began to go purple and his jaw was set, then it started twitching, a sure sign he was about to explode. Something had annoyed him. He violently tore the piece of paper from the clipboard, screwed it up into a ball and hurled it across the briefing room.

It was only then that he found his voice. 'Police by consent? Police by bloody consent? We don't police by consent, we police by fear. Fear of being caught, that's what these bastards understand.' And with that he stormed out. Harry was not yet ready to 'police by consent' regardless of what this briefing item told him. It had been amusing to see Harry throw a tantrum but later, when I'd had time to consider, I came around to his point of view. Perhaps this was the start of political correctness.

Harry also struggled to come to terms with modern technology. This time the police canteen was the scene and the offending contraption a microwave oven. The oven had really been introduced as a way of heating prisoners' meals, which meant that several weeks' supplies could be stored in the freezer. Before this, meals had needed to be purchased separately, from a confectioner or café. But it wasn't long before the oven was being used for heating officers' meals too. Unfortunately, men being men, most of them couldn't be bothered to read the instructions.

Sitting in the canteen one morning having my breakfast,

Harry came in with two eggs and four slices of white bread. It was going to be fried egg sandwiches again today, the same as every early-turn shift for the past twenty-five years. He didn't like change, didn't Harry. Eyeing the brand new microwave with suspicion, he tried the door - it opened, it closed - and fiddled with the on/off button and timer dial. You can't actually see microwaves, can you, so how can you trust them? Unlike me, Harry didn't have one at home but thought that he might like to try it out.

'Dave, can I do my fried eggs in this microwave?'

This was just too good a chance to miss. 'Yes, boss,' I lied. 'You can. Just put them in for three minutes each - six minutes altogether - and they'll be done. The only thing is that they have to cook in their own shell, but that saves washing up later.'

In went Harry's eggs, the timer was set for six minutes and he joined me and my mate Pete at our table to wait for his breakfast. I thought that I'd better make myself scarce before Harry realised what I'd done. So I made my way downstairs and out into the back car park, got into my panda car and was just setting off when Harry threw open the canteen window and yelled: 'Watson you bastard, I'll have you for that.' By all accounts, there were bits of exploded egg all over the place.

I'd had a good laugh at Harry's expense but knew that I ought to try and make amends, after all he was my inspector and I liked him, even if he was crackers. Ten minutes later I returned to the canteen with a bacon and egg sandwich, bought from the local café. He accepted the peace offering but kept up the pretence of being angry. The following day Harry wanted to know if he could toast his bread in the microwave but decided to ask someone other than me.

# 6

✳

# The Iron Lady

MRS McKay was a formidable woman. A Magistrate at Brighouse Court for many years, she had recently become chairman of the bench. This was now *her* court, *her* little domain, and it would be run in the manner that suited *her*.

We were now in the late-1980s and Mrs McKay appeared to model herself on the Prime Minister, the one and only Mrs Margaret Thatcher, or, maybe, it was the other way round. She was every bit as forthright in her views as the Iron Lady and just as uncompromising. She would sit in the centre of the Magistrates bench with another two magistrates either side of her. These two were only really there to make up the numbers. There was never any doubt who would decide the verdicts and sentences to be passed down.

Brighouse Magistrates Court at that time had something of a reputation. It was feared by habitual criminals. If they wanted to be released from prison on bail or were facing a trial and possible imprisonment then they would always try to get their trial moved to a nearby court at Halifax or

Huddersfield. Among local criminals, Brighouse was regarded as a 'hanging court', although I doubt that even Mrs McKay would go quite that far. She was treated with the utmost respect and perhaps even feared by all who crossed her path, whether that be witness, criminal or police officer. Unless your name happened to be David Merchant, that is, a burglar of low intelligence, whom Mrs McKay had the pleasure of sending to prison many times over the years.

Merchant's big problem was that he did not know when to keep his mouth shut. Once, I stood alongside him myself in my role as court officer, a job that entailed ensuring the safety of the court and making sure that Merchant didn't try to escape. In this particular trial, the evidence against him was overwhelming, but throughout he kept mumbling and making comments under his breath which, unfortunately for him, were clearly annoying Mrs McKay.

Whenever a witness or prosecutor gave evidence to prove his guilt, the words 'lying bastard' could be heard, or he would sneer and try to intimidate them. His conduct didn't go unnoticed and at the conclusion Mrs McKay wasted little time in finding him guilty. With her next breath she condemned him to four months in Armley prison. She always managed a smile as she delivered a verdict and today was no exception, before finishing off by telling me to: 'Take him away officer'.

The prisoner was a skinny little runt and I didn't expect any trouble from him as I took hold of his elbow and began to escort him to the rear of the court. It was my intention to place him in a secure holding room where he would be locked until transportation to Armley later that day. We walked towards the doors at the back of the courtroom, with Merchant still muttering and swearing under his breath, but he wanted to show off in front of his mates in the public gallery. So he decided that this time he was going to tell Mrs

McKay what he really thought of her. He had probably been waiting years for this opportunity and wasn't going to let it pass. Going to prison anyway, he doubtless thought he had nothing to lose. It would also give his mates a good chuckle and show that he wasn't scared.

'You can get stuffed, Mrs Kay, you silly old cow,' he shouted.

Well, the courtroom fell silent, waiting to see what her response would be. I stood still and took a firmer grip on Merchant's arm before looking back towards Mrs McKay. He had thrown down the gauntlet and now we would see what Mrs McKay was really made of. After the briefest of pauses, she did not disappoint.

'Officer, please bring that man back into the dock.'

Back we marched and, once again, I stood alongside him. His young, suave and sophisticated solicitor was now a worried man, in an apparent state of near panic, beads of perspiration on his brow. His smart suit and educated voice weren't going to help him out of this mess. This was going to be fun; I do love to see a solicitor squirm, especially when it's in Mrs McKay's court. Merchant was now sulking and looking down at the floor, as Mrs McKay sat patiently awaiting an explanation. The crowd at the back of the court had come suddenly to life. They were enjoying this performance and there was sniggering and suppressed laughter at Merchant's little outburst. I didn't know what to expect next, but it was going to be interesting whatever the outcome. To be honest, I too had found his outburst rather amusing and had to suppress the smile that was threatening to creep across my face.

Merchant's solicitor turned to address the magistrates. He didn't know whether to look Mrs McKay directly in the eye or down at the desk in front of him; a combination of the two left him looking like a frightened rabbit in headlights.

For the next three minutes, he offered the most humble and grovelling apology on behalf of his client but was not going to get away with it that easily. Mrs McKay was now in her element. She leaned forward and said: 'Perhaps Mr Merchant would like to give his apology himself?'

The solicitor turned around to face his client and there was whispering between the two. Maybe now we would hear a hint of regret for the outburst. Merchant's eyes remained focussed on the floor as a reluctant and barely audible 'sorry' was uttered.

'What exactly are you sorry for, Mr Merchant?'

'Sorry for what I said.'

Mrs McKay was determined to have her pound of flesh.

'Speak up young man, I couldn't quite hear you.'

Merchant was forced to repeat the apology, louder this time, and the court was so quiet you could have heard a pin drop. He had now completely lost face in front of all his mates. The solicitor regained composure and also found the courage to speak again. He said: 'May I ask if the Bench would accept Mr Merchant's apology?'

It wasn't really a question, more a plea for mercy and for a few seconds I almost felt sorry for him. He would not have come across this scenario very often while studying for his law degree but this was the real world now, the world of Mrs McKay and clients like Merchant. The solicitor had done his best and put in a credible performance under the circumstances, but now he could do no more than wait for Mrs McKay's response, while no doubt hoping that the ground would open up and swallow them both.

Yet anyone thinking it was all over had misjudged the lady. She cleared her throat and waited until the court fell silent, keen for everyone to hear how she dealt with such outbursts. And then, speaking in a calm but powerful voice: 'Yes, the Bench will accept your apology Mr Merchant...

however due to your conduct this morning you will serve an extra fourteen days in prison for contempt of court. This additional sentence will be served after you have finished your four-month sentence for burglary.'

She fixed her eyes on Merchant and held him in an unwavering stare. She had him beat. She knew it and he knew it, a beaming smile spreading across her face. Mrs McKay had her revenge and was now just mocking him. As I led Merchant away and struggled to keep a straight face, I wondered of now he had finally learned his lesson about messing with this lady.

# 7

\*

# Time to Move On

IT had always been my dream to live in the Yorkshire Dales, or as near to the Dales as I could afford. So, in 1986, I joined a self-build scheme in a village near Skipton. This let me put my trade as a carpenter to good use and I was credited with the hours spent working on the project by a reduction in the cost of the house. The construction and internal carpentry of our new family home took almost two years to complete and, during that time, I continued to work as a policeman in Brighouse.

After a while, however, the burden of having two jobs, working shifts and travelling between my home in Bradford to Brighouse and then the Dales each day began to take its toll. My marriage suffered, leading eventually to my then wife and I increasingly living separate lives under the same roof. And having moved, it became obvious that it was time for a change of work too. My daily commute was over twenty miles in each direction so I applied for a transfer to the Queens Road police station in the Manningham district of Bradford. This was a division on the fringe of the city's red-light area, made infamous by the murderous activities of the Yorkshire Ripper in the 1970s. It had a high ethnic population and numerous large council estates. In a nutshell, it was inner-city stuff and about as far removed as possible from the policing methods adopted in Brighouse.

In fact, on my first day at Manningham, my colleagues were astounded that anyone should actually apply for a transfer there. They thought I was mad for volunteering to work there, yet I quickly settled in and in no time at all felt completely at home.

One reason for that was my friendship with a colleague named Rob, who had been in the police force for several years. Rob was a proper gentleman, sympathetic and non-aggressive, the sort of policeman who would rather offer a kindly word of advice than arrest some young thug terrorising their neighbourhood. Sometimes he just needed a push in the right direction, that's all, and maybe he could have been just a little more confident and assertive.

On one particular day, I could tell that Rob was worried about the sign on a garden gate. 'I hate dogs,' he said. 'And do you know something, I think they can tell. They always go for me. Look, Dave, would you mind if I stayed in the car while you do this?' That would be fine. It didn't really need the two of us to deliver a summons to Arnold Whitely. As long as it was handed to that gentleman in person, by a police officer, it didn't matter if there was one officer or two, but I couldn't see why Rob should get away with sitting in the car while I did all the work. I pushed open the gate and we walked down the footpath towards the stone cottage.

'Come on Rob, you'll be fine,' I said, as he followed me with reluctance. Having approached the house, I knocked on the door. From inside came ferocious barking and a fairly high-pitched bark at that, only a small dog by the sound of it. Rob looked a bit nervous and I noticed that he took a step closer, in fact he was almost hiding behind me when the door opened.

What followed happened so quickly. A small white blur shot out - like a bat out of hell - snarling and showing bared teeth. And not only that, as it ran around the back of my legs, it made straight for Rob. This wasn't funny, well, yes, actually, it was. Very funny indeed and especially when the Jack Russell terrier in question sank its fangs into my fellow officer's backside. 'Aaaghh! Get the bloody thing off me,' he howled. 'Get it off!' Rob spun around and around but the beast hung on, each of its four feet swinging clear of the ground, as it growled and slavered through gritted teeth.

The canine assault could not have lasted for more than ten seconds, but it must have felt more like ten minutes to Rob before the owner belatedly came to his rescue. He bellowed at his dog 'LEAVE' before resorting to brute force by giving the hound a hearty kick with his size-nine boot. The dog yelped but the tactic had the desired effect. It let go of Rob's hind quarters and scurried back into the house. Rob, meanwhile, was hopping up and down and vigorously rubbing the right cheek of his backside. The fabric of his trousers was shot to pieces, saliva was smeared everywhere and shredded fibres hung down in rags.

Arnold Whitely showed no sympathy whatsoever. 'Did tha not see t' sign on t' gate warnin tha about t' dog, or can't coppers read nowadays?' he enquired.

Rob was still hobbling about and trying to hide the tears in his eyes. 'Yes, we can read,' I replied. 'But you weren't likely to come to the garden gate to speak to us if you knew that we were trying to serve you with a summons were you?'

'No, I suppose you're right there,' came his surly reply. 'Any road, what's t' summons for this time?'

I handed him the top copy. 'You might have guessed, Arnold. It's for keeping a dangerous dog. You have to appear in court next Thursday.' I placed my own copy in my jacket pocket as Arnold stepped back into his doorway, the dog now safely out of harm's way. I smiled sheepishly at Rob as we turned to walk back towards the garden gate. I was going to get it in the neck now all right.

'I told you that would happen. I just knew it. You said I'd be fine. Remind me never to trust your judgement again,' he said through teeth as clenched as the little dog's had just been. For his part, Arnold wasn't too happy about receiving the summons but he obviously relished the prospect of Rob having to endure even more pain. 'If I were thee lad, I'd get to t' hospital for a tetanus injection. Tha dunt want infection in thi arse now does tha?' He was enjoying the moment.

'Well, you'll be getting another summons now for letting your dog bite me, won't you," replied Rob, determined to salvage some dignity.

'Don't think so, lad. That's not my dog. It's just a stray. I gave t' last dog away to t' scrap yard after it bit t' postman on his arse an' all.'

After Rob lowered himself very gently into the passenger seat, I drove off and we maintained a dignified silence for about the first thirty seconds until, finally, I could contain myself no longer. I laughed so much that I was almost in tears and had to park at the side of the road or risk crashing the car.

Rob didn't find his predicament quite so amusing. 'Bastard, bastard, bastard,' he cursed, one for each of us I assumed, the dog, Arnold and me. 'You had better take me for that tetanus jab,' he said. And so off we went, heading for a four-hour wait at Bradford Royal Infirmary where, this time, a very large needle would be stuck where the sun refused to shine.

DURING my time at the old Manningham police station, Queens House always put me in mind of the American television programme *Hill Street Blues*. There was a constant buzz of activity about the place. In the middle of the building was the control room, the real nerve centre of the division. This was where the radio operator and his assistant worked. It was also where the station sergeant had his desk and invariably the shift inspector would join them. Being the biggest room by far, it was also where the team congregated between jobs. Officers would find a vacant seat for a bacon sandwich or a brew. If prisoners were detained in the cells or waiting for interview, they could be kept under observation through glass screens.

One night, I was in this room when the radio operator took a telephone call. He covered the mouthpiece with his hand for a moment and turned to me. 'Dave can you and Neil Power turn out to this one, it sounds serious,' he said. 'The caller thinks someone is trying to break into his flat and threatening to murder him.'

As messages go, this sounded about as urgent as it gets. So Neil and I ran outside and sped off in the panda car. While driving, we were directed to Franklin House, a block of council flats on Barkerend Road, in Bradford. Our radio operator was still on the line to the caller and speaking to us at the same time. It was all rather chilling. Apparently, there was a man outside this young man's flat trying to smash the door down and shouting that when he got inside he would kill him. Any delay might have disastrous consequences.

We sped through town and up Barkerend Road before abandoning the car on the main road outside the block of flats. By the time the car had come to a stop, Neil was already out and running towards the main entrance at the communal stairway and I was close behind. Just as we were about to enter, a young man came running across the grass towards us, very distressed and crying uncontrollably. Tears were rolling down his cheeks. He was only a small lad, about eighteen years of age and slightly built, with the face of a boy rather than a man. The poor kid was nearly hysterical and told us that he had made the 999 call. He had been so terrified of the threats shouted through his letter box that he had jumped from his balcony onto the grass below.

Now this may not have been so dramatic were it not for the fact that his flat was on the third floor. This young man had risked his life to escape the madman threatening him. He said that he didn't know who was making the threats or what it was all about but that the man was still there, on the landing, outside the door of his flat.

Telling the young man to wait outside, Neil and I went in and immediately heard the torrent of abuse coming from above. The walls and stairs were all made of concrete and a booming voice echoed through the block. Its owner was clearly unconcerned about anyone else hearing the threats. They were quite specific in that when this man got into the flat he was going to kill the 'fucking bastard' for locking him out. Deciding to get a good look at this bloke before he saw us, we crept quietly upstairs, his voice so intimidating that I wanted more accurately to assess the threat. There was something not quite right about it though. His speech was slurred, he may have been drunk or possibly had a speech impediment. He didn't sound like a young man, probably middle-aged or older. And then, as we approached the third floor landing, I caught sight of him.

He was sitting on the floor, slumped against the door of the flat with his back to us, having not yet sensed our presence. About fifty years old, with grey hair and a couple of days growth of stubble, he wore industrial clothing and had probably gone straight to the pub from work. Either way, I could smell the booze from five yards. He didn't see or hear our approach and I was able to creep up right behind him. Once there, I cupped my hands together in front of my mouth to form an improvised megaphone and leaned forward, so that my hands were only inches from his left ear. Oblivious to all this, I realised that his eyes were actually closed but that his mouth was still working as he continued to shout his threats. I took a deep breath, pushed my mouth close to my cupped hands and bellowed 'be quiet!' as loud as I could directly into his left ear. It had an immediate effect.

Suddenly, the torrent of abuse stopped as he sluggishly turned round and looked directly at me. He had a very puzzled expression on his face, as though he didn't really understand what was happening. He was slumped against the door of the flat because, being dead drunk, he was incapable of standing up. How he had even managed to negotiate the steps up to this level was a miracle and I was sure that he would not be capable of harming anyone.

I allowed a minute or two for the ringing to stop in his ear and then asked why he was shouting. His reply was quite revealing: 'She's locked me out,' he said.

'Who has locked you out?'

'The pissin' wife. And she's changed the pissin' locks so I can't get back in.'

He fumbled about and retrieved the key with which he had been trying to unlock the door, handing it to me. I then noticed the lad who made the complaint hovering nervously on the stairs, listening to the conversation. He took one look at the man who was the cause of his fear and said: 'But this isn't your flat. You live in the next block down.' It was then that the penny dropped. Each block of flats was identical from the outside and the drunk had come to the wrong one, too paralytic to read the name of the building.

# Out of the Blue

The young man was so relieved at no longer being under threat of death that he chose not to make a formal complaint. So we lifted the drunk to his feet before helping him down the stairs and out of the front door. We then sent him on his way, secretly hoping that we wouldn't be seeing him again later on, mired in a domestic dispute.

A JOB that had originally sounded serious had turned out to be fairly lighthearted really, but it reminded me of another job at the same flats only a week earlier which had a very different outcome completely.

I was still tutoring raw recruits and Susan, my latest probationer, was approaching the last few days of training. However, she hadn't yet dealt with a sudden death and that would be seen as an essential requirement before moving on to the next stage, independent patrol. I had already had a word with our radio operator and told him that we would deal with the next sudden death reported. It wasn't a job I relished, but it had to be done for Susan's benefit. I expected her to be nervous and apprehensive about dealing with a dead body, but it was better that it happened when she was with me rather than by herself in only a week's time.

Eventually, we received the call. 'Hotel Alpha One... Are you still wanting to deal with a sudden death?'

'Go ahead, pass us the details.'

He went on to do just that, but it was the last of these that really floored me. 'It's a cot death; baby girl of five months. The mother has found her dead in bed. The ambulance has already been and the doctor called to certify death. He is on his way there now.'

We drove there almost in silence, deep in thought, as we both had young children of our own. Cot deaths are always heartbreaking no matter how many other deaths you have dealt with but, for Susan, going to deal with such an incident for the first time must have been terrifying.

I parked outside the flats and we climbed the concrete stairs to the cold third-floor landing. As we walked along the corridor I turned to Susan and said that I would do all the talking, all she had to do was watch. She nodded without speaking, it was obvious she was already quite emotional and this was going to be tough. I knocked on a bright red wooden door with scratches gouged into the paint. A dog began to bark inside, probably the same one responsible for the scratch marks. A young woman answered and ushered us inside, through the kitchen and into the living room.

'Kathy's upstairs with Lauren. I'll get her for you.'

Her loud footsteps echoed as she climbed the uncarpeted wooden staircase to the bedroom above. While she did so, I looked around at the battered couch and two easy chairs, at the television, video recorder and stereo, at the wooden coffee table with lumps of wood veneer missing on every corner. A unkempt room, in short, in need of a thorough spring clean. And we were stood in the middle of the room when the woman who had answered the door - a friend and neighbour - returned with the still-crying Kathy, who had two black eyes where she had been wiping away the tears and rubbing last night's mascara into her skin.

The story was indeed an upsetting one. Kathy had been out for the evening with friends, leaving a neighbour's teenage daughter to babysit, before coming home at three in the morning, drunk but happy. She'd had a good night out and now just wanted to sleep, so she paid her babysitter and went straight to bed. Lauren, meanwhile, had been asleep in her cot but woke when Kathy came into the bedroom. It was too tempting for the young mother; she wanted to sleep with her lovely baby daughter. Lifting Lauren out of her cot, she laid her in the double bed and climbed in alongside her, too tired or drunk to remove her lipstick and make-up or even her clothing. In seconds, wearing exactly the same outfit that she had been out in, she fell asleep.

It had been lunchtime when Kathy awoke, about two hours before our arrival. Delighted to see that Lauren was still asleep, she slid out of bed and went downstairs to make herself a drink and some breakfast. About an hour later, with Lauren still quiet, Kathy decided that she should go check on her daughter. She was met with a moment to give every mother nightmares. Lauren had not moved. Worse, her face was cold to the touch and she was no longer breathing. But she looked so peaceful, so perfect.

We accompanied Kathy into the bedroom but she immediately walked back out onto the landing. She could not bear to be in there with her dead daughter. As with any sudden or unexplained death, the police have a duty to provide a detailed report surrounding the circumstances to the coroner. This report will assist in the post mortem, so it is vital that it is done thoroughly. The body must be checked therefore for any signs of injury that suggest a crime may have taken place. This was not the case with Lauren. It was as though she had just gone to sleep and stopped breathing.

After the doctor arrived and confirmed that death had occurred, the funeral director took Lauren to the mortuary. He carried her tiny coffin in his arms as he walked along the corridor and down three flights of stairs to his waiting car. The whole process seemed wrong somehow. It was almost indecent and lacking in compassion. I would not be critical of the funeral director but, only the night before, a beautiful healthy baby girl had gone to sleep and not woken up. And now here she was being carried in a little wooden box along a grotty corridor by a stranger in a black suit. Shortly, he would be carrying her down a filthy staircase, putting her in the back of his car and driving away. The sight of it pulled at my heartstrings and, I have to confess, I found it difficult to go through with the process required.

My role was to gather information. I questioned Kathy about Lauren's health, whether she took any medication and the details of the babysitter, so that I could question her too. I also required the details of the neighbour who Kathy first ran to when she discovered Lauren's death. Most traumatic of all was obtaining a precise account of Kathy's actions when she arrived home drunk and placed Lauren in the double bed alongside her. I had to seize the bedding as police exhibits and interview Kathy under caution.

The post mortem revealed that Lauren had died as a result of being accidentally smothered. Apparently, this is not uncommon when a baby shares a bed with an adult who is under the influence of alcohol. There is even an official name for such a death: roll-over. Kathy had smothered her own child by rolling onto her while asleep. It was just a silly mistake and I had to ask myself what parent hasn't slept with their baby at some point.

The diverse nature of these two jobs in the same location typified the role of a police officer. Two very different incidents, just seven days apart, one light-hearted, one tragic... same policeman.

# 8

*

## Challenging Times

MANNINGHAM, Bradford. It's nearly 2.00am on a Friday
night - Saturday morning, but so far so good. Once again I
am partnered with Neil and although we'd expected to be
busy, all is relatively calm: a couple of kids missing from the
Local Authority children's home, run-of-the-mill stuff really,
nothing to get too excited about. No doubt we would fill in
the reports back at the station so that their descriptions
could be circulated the length and breadth of the nation,
only for the little blighters to return safe and well in the
morning having 'missed the last bus home' or 'spent the
night at a friend's'.

On top of that, we'd had a nice slice of luck. Around half
an hour earlier, officers in a road traffic car volunteered to go
to a crash that sounded quite serious. It was on our patch
and we could easily have been roped in ourselves, spending
hours on point duty while the traffic lads sat in their cars
dealing with the paperwork. Soon, though, it *was* our turn.
The radio blurted out our call sign: 'Hotel Alfa Two, can you

attend Gaisby Mills? There has been a jumper from the top of the mill chimney.'

Well, that's something a bit different, we thought. The chimney on Gaisby Mills must be two hundred feet high. Anyone jumping from the top of there must surely be dead by now. In any case, we sped along Canal Road and through Bolton Woods before turning into the mill yard, eventually pulling in directly behind the attending ambulance. Surely an undertaker's van would be more appropriate.

As we came to a stop, a man came racing towards us, waving his arms above his head, clearly in a state of absolute panic. 'It's Billy,' he said. 'He's fallen off the chimney'. Our witness then turned on his heels and ran towards the back of the mill, beckoning us to follow. He told us that his name was Mike and I couldn't help but notice that he was having difficulty running in a straight line. He was also slurring his words. There was more to this than met the eye.

As Neil and I followed Mike around the back of the main building, the elderly ambulance crew struggled to keep up, lagging behind. And soon, it was pitch black. He had led us into an alley that separated the mill from a substantial stone warehouse. The place looked as if it had been used for years as a dumping ground by the various small businesses which now occupied the complex. Ahead of us, in the darkness, we could just about make out a three-foot mound of debris; old tyres, bits of carpet, wooden pallets and cast-off mattresses. We clambered over all this rubbish and continued to trail Mike, who beckoned us further into the alleyway.

'Billy, Billy, we're coming,' he yelled, apparently trying to locate his friend. By now, it was increasingly obvious just how drunk Mike was and I began to wonder whether this might be a practical joke of some sort. Looking up, the mill chimney towered high above us, stretching all the way into the moonlit sky, but Mike remained undeterred and kept howling to his mate. It was tough going. Feet that didn't get stuck in tyres cracked through sheets of plywood that had long seen better days. The stench of rotting garbage made breathing unpleasant to say the least.

Mike continued to shout Billy's name but, for the rest of us, frustration had by now crept in. Why couldn't he find his mate when he claimed to have seen him fall off the chimney? Was Mike really an escapee from a psychiatric ward somewhere who had imagined the whole thing? Then, in between the desperate calls, we heard a faint groan.

Remarkably, as we moved slowly forward, the top of Billy's head did indeed come into view. He was laying in a crumpled heap, half submerged beneath piles of God knows what. If he actually had tumbled from the chimney then, it seemed reasonable to assume, all of this garbage must have somehow broken his fall. One of his legs was buried under rubbish and the other was twisted at a strange angle. He had landed on his back but his neck was bent forward to such a degree that his chin was wedged tight against his chest. Barely conscious, he failed to respond when spoken to. Fearing that his friend was going to die and in between bouts of drunken sobbing, Mike finally revealed what had occurred.

The two of them had been drinking in their local pub and then embarked upon their short walk home. En route, Billy confessed that one of his long-held ambitions was to climb right to the top of the iron ladder affixed to the Gaisby Mills chimney. The only problem was that it didn't extend all the way to ground level, but Billy had been thinking about this for some time and he had a plan. If the pair were to climb the metal fire escape on the warehouse opposite, they could gain access to the warehouse roof. From there, they could dive across the alleyway and, with arms outstretched, would be able to grab hold of the bottom rung of the iron ladder.

Having made this almighty leap of faith, they would then ascend their way to either the top of said mill chimney or, more likely, heaven.

Of such ingenuity is drunken ambition made. And that's leaving aside the fact that although the jump from the warehouse roof to the ladder would be downhill - and therefore just about achievable for a brave and sober acrobat in broad daylight - the return leap would be upward and virtually impossible. But they hadn't yet thought about that.

Fortunately, the ambulance crew were able to return with a stretcher just as Billy began to regain consciousness. His neck, he complained, was hurting like hell. And again, Mike explained why. Together, the two men had climbed the fire escape and approached the edge of the warehouse roof ready to make the leap. It was Billy's idea, so he would go first. Duly, the human spiderman lunged across the eight-foot chasm before gravity took its course and he made a rapid descent. Mike, looking on, was horrified as his pal hurtled to earth like a stone, before striking his head on an air conditioning unit bolted to the side of the mill, twisting in mid-air and hitting the ground. After scampering back down the fire escape, Mike called for an ambulance and then waited in the mill yard to flag us down.

Although the ambulance crew had indeed now rejoined us with their stretcher, they were puffing and panting like Dad's Army, after twice clambering over those mountains of trash. How the heck would they manage to carry Billy out? The highly-trained paramedics whose job this would usually have been were at the traffic incident that we had been so clever in avoiding. How I now wished that we had attended that one instead. These couple of old boys were not much more than glorified taxi drivers but they were the best on offer and carried out an assessment of Billy's injuries, before deciding that he probably had a broken neck.

## Out of the Blue

Needless to say, moving Billy onto the stretcher without moving his spine or neck was a struggle to say the least. His little team of rescuers consisted of two elderly ambulance drivers, a couple of policemen who knew little about first aid and Mike, who was both pissed and distraught. His job would be to try and keep Billy talking. A slow and difficult process, then, especially when the 'ground' was constantly shifting beneath our feet. Thirty minutes later, though, he was finally ready for an equally bumpy ride out of the alley, strapped down with crepe bandages to prevent him falling off. Once in the ambulance, he was driven to Bradford Royal Infirmary.

There, Billy was rushed straight to the treatment room where he continued to complain that his only pain was from his neck and head as the booze began to wear off. For our part, Neil and I had also gone to the hospital in order to get Billy's details, so that we could then notify his wife as to his injuries. Upon being removed from the stretcher and placed on a trolley, Billy turned to Neil and said: 'Excuse me, mate. My head is killing me, will you put that pillow under it?' So Neil, always obliging, did so. He put one hand under Billy's head and lifted it up, picked up the pillow with his other hand and shoved it in place. I was just about to say: 'No, don't move his head, he's got a broken neck,' but I was too late. 'Thanks, mate. That's better,' said Billy. I remained silent. Some things are best left unsaid.

A couple of months later, I was driving through Bolton Woods when I saw Billy pushing himself up the road in a wheelchair. He was just leaving the pub and making his way home. Old habits die hard. I couldn't help but wonder if he was in that wheelchair because of his fall or because of the incident with Neil and the pillow, and I guess I will never know. Within a year I bumped into Mike too and asked him about his mate. Apparently, Billy was now fully recovered and back at work on a building site. Happily, he had now given up on his ambition to climb the mill chimney.

DEALING with death can be almost as common for some police officers as dealing with criminals is for others. And for uniform patrol officers it just cannot be avoided. A police officer is sent to all sudden or unexplained deaths, to act for the Coroner's Officer and to submit a report outlining the circumstances. There is also an element of 'hands on' with the deceased. It is essential that the body is examined for any sign of injury that may have contributed to the fatality. The only way to do that properly is by examination and even touching of the body. Personal possessions such as clothing and jewellery have to be removed and handed over to the next of kin.

Many officers never come to terms with this unpleasant aspect of policing. I have known colleagues who resigned or requested transfers to other departments in order to avoid handling dead bodies. Like most people, I never relished the prospect of sudden death but, over time, thought that I had grown used it and seen everything there was to see, whether that be the tragedy of a cot death or a decomposed old man who had lain lonely and undiscovered for weeks. Yes, I felt myself experienced in these matters, but what happened in 1993 made me think again.

At the time, I was on the beat in the Gilstead area of Bingley. The area in question is quite a large residential area and a large part of my work took me to three huge council tower blocks, ten storeys high, each containing almost one hundred flats. Notoriously, these towers housed a number of criminals and otherwise less-than-desirable tenants.

In fact, their only saving grace were the caretakers, two of whom were great friends, having worked there for years.

# Out of the Blue

There wasn't much that went on in these tower blocks that was missed by Doris and Harriet. If one of them failed to spot something, the other was sure to tell her about it. These ladies lived in separate blocks but shared their daily work of mopping and cleaning the stairways, lifts and corridors. In fact, they almost lived in each other's pockets. As a result, they were a great source of information for me. They always knew who was living where and with whom. They knew who drove which car and at what time of day and night they usually came and went. Of course, I couldn't hope to obtain such news without sitting down with the ladies and sharing a cup of tea and a plate of biscuits.

After six months or so, I had begun to regard Doris and Harriet as friends rather than just ordinary members of the public. We would often talk about our families and holidays, or of our interests outside work. If they had any problems with the tenants, I became the first person they would turn to. These two ladies were no longer just the caretakers of the flats, they were people who were important to me, people I cared about.

I had just left the police station one morning when a radio message informed me that Doris had phoned, saying she wanted to see me. There was nothing to suggest any urgency, so I walked the short distance to the estate and knocked on the door of her flat. When she answered it, she was crying and in a terrible state, shaking and unable to speak clearly between the sobs. Eventually, though, she did manage to tell me that Harriet hadn't come round to join her that morning. She had a key for Harriet's flat but couldn't gain entry as there was something wedged behind the door, preventing it from opening.

If Doris suspected that it was Harriet's body behind the door she wasn't saying, but that is exactly what it turned out to be. When I took the key from Doris and tried to open the door myself, the lock turned but the door was indeed wedged tightly shut. I pushed harder and it gave a little, so I pushed a little more until there was just enough room to squeeze my head through. I looked down at the floor and there, as expected, was Harriet's body in a crumpled heap, but it was still a shock. Poor Harriet. She lived alone and might well have been like this all night.

Eventually, I managed to push the door wide enough to get my whole body through, but I didn't want to push too hard as it seemed disrespectful to Harriet, even though I was sure she was already dead. I crouched down beside her and felt for a pulse in her wrist. Nothing. I watched carefully to see if there was any breathing, any rise or fall of the chest. Nothing. My heart was racing and I struggled to keep calm. What on earth was wrong with me? I hadn't felt this tense since dealing with my first ever body. I began to talk to myself, to try to calm myself down, going over what had to be done. Firstly, contact a doctor to certify death. Secondly, contact the funeral directors, who will take her to the mortuary. Thirdly, check the premises to make sure that no one had broken in and killed her. Finally, check her body for injuries and signs of violence.

I was a bundle of nerves and glad that no one was there to see me in such a state. I went to pieces because, for the first time in a decade, I had not only found the deceased, I'd had to deal with the death of someone I considered to be a friend. It knocked me for six and it was some time before I regained my usual composure.

Harriet's death turned out to be from natural causes. She had died of a sudden heart attack and it was left to me to inform her son. He was aged about twenty-five and I had only met him occasionally at his mother's flat but it was still an upsetting task for all concerned. A couple of days later he phoned me at work and asked if I would attend Harriet's funeral, which was to take place the following week. I said I would love to do so but that I would be working on that day, so I would have to see if I could get some time off.

His next comment both surprised and delighted me. He said that because Harriet had only ever known me as a policeman her family would be honoured if I would attend in full uniform and salute her coffin as it was brought into the crematorium.

I answered that it would be a privilege to carry out that task. It touched me deeply how, sometimes, one's life as a police officer can become so closely entwined with the people you meet in the course of your duty.

# 9

**\***

# Game for a Laugh?

SHIPLEY had been a thriving sub-divisional headquarters, a purpose-built police station with facilities that were the envy of larger and better known divisions. It had its own cells, CID and traffic departments, a communications room - where a radio operator could be found twenty-four hours a day - and an enquiry desk that was also open around the clock for the benefit of the general public. In charge of this efficient yet rather homely station was a superintendent, ably assisted by several inspectors and civilian staff.

At least, this was how I found Shipley police station when I first transferred there from Bradford in 1993. Sadly, however, everything was about to change and I'm afraid it was not a change for the better.

Big is beautiful. Well, that is clearly what the Chief Constable believed, sitting in his ivory tower at Wakefield HQ. Divisional boundaries needed to be altered, personnel moved around. Huge divisions would be created, to which hundreds of officers would be posted. Unfortunately, these new bigger police divisions turned out to be isolated and remote from the communities which they were supposed to protect. It was the death knell for small town stations such as Shipley and many others like it.

As part of the overhaul, Shipley was to become part of a new Eccleshill division in Bradford. A distance of only three miles separated these two places, but they both required a completely different way of policing. Eccleshill is in an inner city, urban area, containing several large council estates. Shipley, on the other hand, is an independent small town. The prison cells at Shipley were closed first. Then the CID and traffic departments were moved to Bradford, with their senior officers given posts elsewhere. But there was one change that the people of Shipley simply would not accept.

For the past forty years, these people could walk into their local police station at any time of day or night and speak to an officer on the enquiry desk. This was convenient if they were out shopping or worked in the town centre; there were even parking facilities outside the front door. Yet now, that too would be taken away. The enquiry desk was to close, replaced by a bright yellow telephone fixed to the wall outside. Callers would no longer speak face to face to a local bobby, they would be put through to a communications centre at Wakefield, over twenty miles away.

Two incidents occurred within the space of a few weeks that may have left the Chief Constable wishing he had given a little more consideration to his masterplan. The first was on a Saturday night, a time when the police station was now completely deserted, despite a press release that deliberately misled the public stating it was still manned twenty-four hours a day. This wasn't true. Officers who went on duty at Shipley at ten o'clock were out on patrol within ten minutes. The last to leave the building simply locked the door behind him and set the burglar alarm.

On this particular evening, Thomas, a local man, was having a night out on the town. As sometimes happens, he had too much to drink and got into an argument with a gang of youths. The argument got out of hand and was about to turn into a street fight which, quite obviously, Thomas expected to lose since he was outnumbered by around five to one. As a last resort he sought sanctuary at Shipley police station, or at least that was his intention as he began running in that direction along Manor Lane.

Yet what did he find when he got there? Bounding up the half-dozen steps outside he was horrified to find the front door locked and the building in darkness. Desperately, he banged on the door and shouted for help at the top of his voice, convinced that there must be police officers inside the building and that they would come to his aid. The chasing gang was nearly upon him. He had to do something quickly or else be kicked senseless right where he stood, on the steps of the police station. As his anxiety got the better of him, he began to kick at the door and did so with such force that the casing splintered and the door swung open. He ran inside, seeking refuge, but that wasn't going to put this gang off, they were after his blood.

Thomas ran along the main corridor screaming for help and pursued by the gang of thugs. He ducked into several offices, all of them deserted. And so, in one final act of desperation, he picked up a telephone and dialled 999. He wanted the emergency services, he needed the police but no one answered the call. What Thomas hadn't realised was that the first nine only gave the caller an outside line. What he really needed to dial was 9999. He was now cornered, with no way out. The gang surrounded him and beat him to the floor. Then they took the opportunity to wreck havoc by throwing papers and computers around the rooms.

Unwittingly, however, by breaking into the station

## Out of the Blue

Thomas had activated the burglar alarm. This sent a taped message to the control room at Bradford and I was sent to investigate. Upon my arrival, I found the gang long gone and Thomas covered in blood, needing to go to hospital and feeling totally let down by the police when he had needed their help most. To add to his woes, he had to be arrested for damaging the station doors but, fortunately, the senior officers saw sense and he wasn't prosecuted.

Needless to say, this was an embarrassing incident for the police force and one which it would have preferred to brush under the carpet, but it wasn't going to be that easy.

Within weeks of the new door being fitted a second and similar incident took place. This time, a vehicle had been stopped by road traffic officers in Baildon, only a mile or so from the station. The car in question had been stolen only minutes earlier and its two occupants were put under arrest, but it was important to find the complainant to confirm that the vehicle was, in fact, stolen. I was sent to the scene of the burglary and saw that the house was insecure. The burglars had broken in, stolen the car keys and then gone about their business. Enquiries with neighbours produced a mobile number for the car's owner, Kevin, believed to be having a night out in Shipley with his wife. I called Kevin and, sure enough, he was in a very noisy nightclub. I gave him the bad news but he didn't believe me, sounded drunk and, thinking it was a practical joke by a mate, switched his telephone off.

It was only when he left the nightclub and arrived home that he realised my phone call had been genuine. His door *was* boarded up and he *had* been burgled. Jumping in a taxi, he headed straight for the police station at Shipley only to discover, like Thomas, that the front door was locked. He too banged on the door but got no response. With the taxi now gone, he tried the yellow telephone on the outside wall. This put him through to the operator in Wakefield who wanted to know his name, address, telephone number and other details. At this, Kevin lost his temper and said that as he had just been phoned by the police, they must surely already know all his details.

He slammed the phone down and decided to deal with the matter in his own way. First, he kicked open the newly replaced door and once again set off the alarm. Then he walked to the sliding windows that separated the public area from the enquiry officer's desk, stuck a clenched fist through the glass and attempted to alert anyone inside with a shout. By now, Kevin was convinced that the officers were in hiding, no doubt drinking tea and watching telly. The real reason he got no response, of course, was because everyone was out on patrol. The building was deserted but he wasn't convinced.

Kevin was determined that he would find these skivers. He decided to climb through the gap where the glass had once been and search the rest of the offices for himself. Of shorter than average height but possessed of a larger than average waist, however, he was too large to fit through the gap in front of him. Somehow, he managed to get his feet off the floor and push his head and shoulders through, but his ample midriff soon got well and truly stuck. He couldn't go forward and he couldn't go back. His feet were hanging free but couldn't reach the floor, so there wasn't anything to push or pull against. He began to shout for help, time and time again. And he was still yelling his head off when another pair of officers finally arrived, sent to investigate the burglar alarm which had once more been activated. Kevin was eventually released from his self-inflicted incarceration and duly arrested for causing criminal damage.

Again, the senior management didn't want any adverse publicity about people seeking help from a deserted police station that was still officially open, so there was to be no prosecution. Could it be that the Chief Constable had never worked in a town like Shipley?

ONE summer evening, while working in Shipley, I was sent to a council flat in Windhill. A 999 call had requested an ambulance, or at least the operator in the control room reported that a male voice had been heard asking for help. When he tried to return the call, however, the telephone had been left off the hook and so the problem was passed on to the police. Not surprisingly, given those scant details, when we arrived some time before the ambulance we had no idea what to expect.

The flat was on the second floor of the building. I knocked and tried the handle but the door was locked, and this door would be the only means of entry as the windows were high above ground level. I knocked again and when I still got no reply shouted through the letter box. Silence. As a matter of procedure, the person who made the emergency call would have to be seen and spoken to, ensuring that they were fit and well. Despite the locked door and lack of response we couldn't walk away until that was confirmed. There was only one thing left to do - force entry. I asked the radio operator to send another police car and stressed that the officers should first call at the police station to collect the door ram, a large and heavy tool specifically made for the emergency services. We waited patiently for ten minutes or so until our fellow officers and the door ram arrived before, a couple of minutes after that, smashing our way in.

The first thing to hit us was the temperature; the central heating was at full blast. The four of us walked along the corridor shouting that we were the police, but there was no response. Someone must be home and surely they would have heard the racket we made in breaking apart their door.

Maybe someone was ill or unconscious. We continued to move cautiously along the corridor until we came to the living room. And there we were met with the most bizarre of sights, one which left us completely lost for words.

Laid on the floor of the lounge was a man of about thirty years of age, trussed up with black leather straps around his ankles and knees. His arms were fastened behind his back and his wrists tied together. His head was covered with black leather and his mouth was gagged, presumably to stop him from talking. I don't speak from personal experience, but I understand that these items are usually referred to as gimp masks.

On top of all that, he was fastened, from behind, to a five-foot steel scaffold pipe which was itself passed through all the leather straps that bound him. This pipe prevented him from moving any of his limbs or even bending at the waist. It appeared that before we arrived he had originally been propped up on a chair. We worked out that he had then deliberately tipped the chair over so that he could fall onto the floor. This was the only possible way he could use his nose to press 999 on his telephone handset and get help. Nor were the straps that tied his arms and legs to the scaffold pole normal leather straps. They were manufactured in such a way that, after they had been pulled tight and fastened, there was a loop that clipped into a small padlock. Each strap had a padlock to prevent it from being unfastened but how did we know where the key - or keys - were?

The four of us stood over this unfortunate fellow not really knowing what was expected of us. There was no one else in the flat, so we would have to release him somehow. I tried speaking to him but his face mask and mouth gag prevented any response and he looked away as if trying to ignore us. We rolled him over onto his back to try and remove the mask and then I saw a sight that was, if it were possible, even more alarming. The front of his jeans were unfastened and his private parts were completely exposed. A closer look - but not too close - revealed that he had an electric cable wrapped tightly around his penis and testicles. Where the cables came into contact with his skin, the bright red plastic insulation had been stripped back and the bare metal wires were in direct contact with this most delicate part of any man's anatomy. I was intrigued to see what was attached to the other end, as it snaked along the floor and went out of sight under the kitchen table. Crouching down for a look, I was astounded to discover that the cable was attached to the terminals of a heavy duty battery power pack. This must have been giving him a constant electric shock to his scrotum. Talk about being turned on!

Determined to work out what this was all about, we eventually managed to remove his mask and mouth gag although, perhaps understandably, he did seem reluctant to be drawn into conversation. We explained that we couldn't open the padlocks to free him as we didn't have the keys. He glanced at the ceiling and muttered something about a light fittings. Sure enough, there was a small ice cube hanging down where he had indicated, attached by a piece of string frozen into the ice. This ice cube was melting. Water was dripping onto the carpet and a small padlock key was clearly visible inside. As I said, bizarre.

It didn't take long for the heat in the room to melt the ice and allow us to retrieve the key. One by one we opened the padlocks and removed the leather straps. As we freed the man's arms he turned his back and sheepishly removed the electric cable from his testicles. He probably realised that we had no intention of doing that for him. We then unlocked the padlocks on his legs before turning off the heating and opening a window to cool the place down.

Asked for an explanation, our 'victim' said that he had

tied himself up, although it would have been impossible for him to do so with no one else involved, as he claimed. For example, someone must have turned the heating onto its highest setting in order to melt the ice cube more quickly. Each padlock was fastened behind his back, yet he would open them with the key and do all of this when his hands were securely fastened together?

On the table was a German pornographic magazine, open on a two-page spread, depicting a scene almost identical to the one that we saw on first entering the room. No doubt, he had tred to copy this scene for his own sexual gratification but, at some stage, had panicked and tapped out 999 with his nose. Finding himself in this frightening and embarrassing situation, he probably hoped for a couple of mature ambulance drivers and that they would be professional and discreet about his predicament.

Unfortunately for him, he got a quartet of childish and sniggering policemen who not only asked him lots of very embarrassing questions, they completely trashed the door of his flat to gain entry and then went back to the police station to share tales of his exploits with their colleagues.

# 10

*

# Heroin: Paying the Price

LAYTON DOUGLAS shuffles from foot to foot. Left foot...
right foot... he is agitated, unable to remain still. His cheeks
are flooded in tears and snot, which he wipes away with his
shirt sleeve. He tries sitting down, but is soon rocking back
and forth again in the face of the doctor's questions. Yes, he
has taken heroin recently. That was three days ago, what day
is it today? The answer is Saturday and we are in the
medical room of Eccleshill Police Station in Bradford.

Layton tells the doctor that he is currently on methadone,
a heroin substitute prescribed to addicts. But the amount
isn't enough to sort him out, he says, and is reduced day by
day as part of the conditions controlling his prescription.

He also tells the doctor about Chloe, his childhood
sweetheart. Not yet twenty years old, Layton has shared a
home with Chloe for five years. He speaks of their daughter,
Danielle, now thirteen months, and his pain is tangible as he
again starts sobbing and, for the next few minutes, is unable
to continue.

Eventually, Layton regains a little composure and goes on to relate how, in January, he had returned to the couple's council flat only to find Chloe laying in bed, cold and still, taken from him by an overdose of heroin probably supplied by a friend named Paul. And then, no sooner had he buried Chloe than social services took Danielle away and put her in the care of her Godparents. No visits would be allowed until his heroin habit was kicked. His home was then demolished as part of a slum clearance initiative; the whole area had become a centre for addicts and burglars. Soon, Layton was homeless and finding a bed for the night wherever he could. His life was on a downward spiral.

In this, he was following the same route as so many young men of his generation; committed to a life of petty crime in order to feed a drug habit and destined for the complete emotional breakdown he is now suffering before us. 'You know me, don't you, Mr Watson?' he says. 'This isn't me, is it? Tell the doctor that there's something wrong with me.' A lad who I feel desperately sorry for and who I have watched growing up over the last few years is pleading for my help, but I struggle to find the words to comfort him.

The doctor asks Layton if he has ever tried to harm himself. He replies that three days ago he had somehow lost all his clothing and proceeded to walk the streets naked. He recently took lots of tablets to end it all, he adds, before going on to state with some resentment that: 'I died once, but the doctors brought me back and made me live.' He was asked about his feelings for Danielle and whether he would ever harm her. It had been suggested on his medical records that this was a possibility. 'I just don't know,' he answers truthfully, before placing the palms of his hands over his ears and squeezing hard as if trying to shut out the doctor's voice or maybe the voices in his own head. 'Half of me says I should end it all and that me and Danielle should be with

Chloe, but the other half says I've got to get better so I can be a proper parent.'

And then he is crying again; no screams or wails, just uncontrollable sobbing. He tells of how he has spent the previous wet autumn night at the side of Chloe's grave, in a cemetery on the other side of the city, and the evidence for this is right there before us. His clothing is dirty and damp. He turns to the doctor and asks if he is going to get better. The doctor says 'I hope so', which seems so inadequate.

With the medical examination over, I am asked to return Layton to a cell until the local psychiatric hospital has been contacted. Instead I take him outdoors to the exercise yard where he is allowed to smoke and I fetch him a cup of tea. In recent years I have dealt with this young man on a number of occasions and he doubtless regards me as a friend. He confides in me further, about an incident only last week.

Layton had been behind the wheel of a car when he saw the aforementioned Paul and an unknown female walking along the road. For a brief moment, he had contemplated running them over and destroying their lives just as Paul had destroyed his, but the pair had a child with them, which might just have saved their lives. For instead of ploughing into this little family, Layton instead drove past and parked in a nearby quarry, where he promptly burst into tears. Paul, meanwhile, walked on, oblivious to the devastation brought to bear on Layton, Chloe and Danielle.

At the end of my shift that day back in 1997, I returned home but found it impossible to let go of Layton's plight. My home was safe, warm and comfortable. My wife and children were in bed, secure and content, maybe looking forward to our next holiday or some other treat. But what did Layton have in store? A lifetime of misery, most likely, and probably a short one at that. Even today, I don't feel guilty about my lifestyle but it does disturb me more than I may care to admit. I have been a part of a system that has failed lads like Layton. In his case, I saw him change from a kid who got up to childish pranks, to one who indulged in petty crime and then descended into the disastrous twilight zone of hard drugs. And that could so easily happen to my own kids. I've witnessed it first hand with other policemen's children, so I know that no one is immune.

Every police officer has to find a way of dealing with life's traumas. Years ago, I found a way that worked for me. It seemed to exorcise the ghost of utter despondency and hopelessness which at times can be overwhelming. I began to write down my innermost thoughts, to make a written record so that all the despair was no longer just stored within my head. Doing this provided me with a sort of inner sanctuary and it felt like I was sharing the burden I carried within me. And yet I didn't want to, or was perhaps unable, to share these thoughts with anyone else. The finished articles would be placed somewhere safe and out of sight, usually hidden within one of my hardback climbing books. I was sure that no one else in the family would consider opening those pages. What follows is one such piece that I found by chance when I started to write these memoirs. It may be nearly fifteen years old but, upon reading it again, the events it describes seem like only yesterday.

> SHE woke up slowly, almost gently, but something was amiss. She felt her left arm being shaken but it was the middle of the night and she should have been alone in the house. She was shaken again, it wasn't a dream. And then she opened her eyes and saw him. Well, she thought it was a man. Couldn't tell really.
> 'What do you want,' she murmured.

'Where's the safe?'

It was a man's voice. His face was covered with a black balaclava, only two slits for his eyes. In fact, he was all in black. Black sweater, black pants, black leather gloves. She couldn't see his shoes yet. He was knelt down at the side of her bed, feet below her line of sight.

'What's your name?' he asked.

'It's Joan. Joan Carr. Who are you?'

'Doesn't matter who I am. Just tell me where the safe is and you won't get hurt.'

Joan Carr lived alone in a detached bungalow on the outskirts of Bradford. Many years ago, it had been a desirable area in which to live but the run-down inner-city had spread into the suburbs and was now less than half a mile away from her home. Joan had lived here for nearly forty years and considered herself too old to move, despite the constant nagging from her children. This was the home she had shared with her husband until his death nine years ago and, although it was now much too big for her, she had every intention of staying put.

The night before, Joan had gone to bed before ten o'clock, read her book for a while and then fallen soundly asleep. She had still been in that deep sleep when the burglar awoke her.

'I don't understand what you mean,' she said. 'I haven't got a safe.'

The intruder looked down at her and then got to his feet feeling frustrated. He had gained entry by forcing open the kitchen window at the back of the house. The wooden window frame had begun to rot and offered little resistance to his jemmy. Climbing inside, he had started his search without the need to turn on any lights as he had come prepared, with a small torch in his pocket. He hadn't intended to disturb the old lady to begin with; he had hoped to locate the safe alone first. Moving from room to room, he removed pictures from walls but there was no sign of any wall safe. Then he began to pull back the corners of carpets, but was left frustrated by the absence of a floor safe too.

So, after twenty minutes, he decided to wake up the owner earlier than planned. After all, she looked quite old and frail, so that wouldn't be much of a risk. His appearance was deliberately menacing as that was the image he would need to project as he frightened her into revealing, first, the whereabouts to a safe that he remained convinced was in the house somewhere and, next, the key and combination number. Having come out of prison only four weeks ago, he had to feed his drug habit somehow.

'Get out of bed,' he said. 'You're coming with me. You are going to show me where the safe is, or wherever else you have stashed your money.'

Joan eased herself up in bed. She struggled to a sitting position and asked the burglar to pass her zimmer frame. 'I can't walk without it... unless you want to carry me.'

Eventually, after going through her sitting room, dining room and spare bedrooms, Joan managed to convince the intruder that she had been telling the truth, there was no safe. Still, it was three in the morning and he needed cash for his dealer; he had to have heroin tonight.

So, in growing desperation, he took her into the kitchen and raided two ten pound notes and some loose change from her purse.

'Would you like a cup of tea and some chocolate cake?' Joan asked.

The burglar was taken by surprise. 'What are you talking about?'

She repeated the question.

'Have you any coffee? I'll have a cup of coffee,' he said, sitting down at the table while Joan made tea for herself and coffee for her visitor. With the kettle boiled, she handed him a cup, as promised, and a slice of chocolate cake. Which, of course, meant that he now had a problem. For how could he eat and drink while wearing a balaclava? He didn't know it yet, but he had seriously misjudged this lady.

Convinced that he was still being cautious by keeping his gloves on - there was no way he would be leaving any fingerprints for the police to find - and deciding that his victim was too old to recall his facial features, he saw no harm in removing his balaclava. She would forget what he looked like in a couple of hours, wouldn't she? And so off came the mask as he got stuck into the coffee and cake, as the unusual twosome sat like a couple of old friends.

The superficially amiable mood did not last long, however. Joan's burglar may have given up on the safe but he still needed to escape with something valuable and easily transported that his dealer would take instead of cash.

So they returned to her bedroom where he rifled through the dressing table and discovered a jewellery box. That would do for a start but he had also noticed the rings on Joan's fingers.

'Take them off,' he ordered.

Joan tried to do as she was told and made to pull off a signet ring, but it was tight over the knuckle and she had to twist it forcefully to get it off. She hardly gave it a second look as she handed it over.

'And the others. I want them all.'

'I can't get my wedding ring and engagement ring off,' she said. 'They've been on my finger for over fifty years.'

'Well, just try. If *you* can't get them off, then I'll do it.'

Joan made pretence of struggling to remove them; she didn't want to give them up unless she had to. 'No, it's no good. They won't come free.'

The burglar grabbed at her left hand and began to twist the rings. They were tight, as Joan said, but he didn't care. His rough treatment tore her skin but still he twisted and pulled before eventually forcing them off. Despite her pain and fear, Joan sat on the bed staring at her attacker, making a mental note of everything about him. She knew his height, his build, the colour of his hair and eyes. She had noticed a tiny scar above his left eyebrow and self-inflicted tattoo on his right wrist. She would later recall his hollow cheeks, prominent nose, discoloured teeth; one of them blackened on account of a dead nerve. She would remember his pale, sallow complexion, the beads of perspiration on his brow and upper lip and the way he sniffed loudly and annoyingly every ten seconds or so.

She wanted to cry and could feel the tears welling up in her eyes but wouldn't allow that to happen. She had a job to do. His negligence and overconfidence had made him vulnerable, she didn't have to go on being his victim. She was too busy memorising every detail of this despicable man to feel sorry for herself.

At long last, the intruder departed, leaving Joan with these final instructions: 'Sit there and don't ring the police or anybody else for at least twenty minutes. If you do I'll be watching.'

And so, after waiting for what must have seemed like an eternity, she finally rang 999.

Being the first officer to arrive, I made a quick search of the gardens and nearby streets but the burglar was gone. And soon, other officers and neighbours arrived to hear her quietly relate the entire incident. I have taken statements from hundreds if not thousands of crime victims over the years, but no one ever had the presence of mind or powers of recollection as that eighty-five year old lady. The sharpness of her intellect made me feel quite inadequate; if had I been in her position I would have been unable to recall the details as accurately as she did.

Her description was in fact so accurate that within days a suspect was arrested. He denied the allegation and an ID parade was arranged at Bradford Central Police station, where Joan once again faced her attacker. This time, however, it was him who was afraid. She walked down the line of potential suspects before looking her cowardly tormentor directly in the eye, thereby condemning him to seven years' imprisonment.

# 11

\*

# No Two Days the Same

ONCE, while on patrol near Shipley, I heard a radio message saying that a man was smashing the windows of a terraced house in Saltaire with a frying pan. Now normally, neither I nor anyone else would expect to find such behaviour there. Named after the famous Victorian industrialist Sir Titus Salt, Saltaire is a World Heritage Site and grand old place, visited by thousands of tourists each year. Its 'cottages' sit side by side on narrow streets. All the neighbours know one another and so such violent incidents are all but unheard of.

The message went on to say that another man had then come out of the house brandishing a carving knife, chasing the first man away. My first impression was that a couple of lunatics must have escaped from the asylum - and that turned out to be a pretty fair description of events. At first, however, all seemed rather strange until my friend Sergeant Karl Everett came on the scene. Karl quickly got to work on the incident and passed details over the radio of one of the men involved. As I was on patrol in the area, Kevin told me to look out for my old mate, Jack Horner. Jack was the man suspected of breaking the windows of the cottage and then running away, only minutes before Karl had attended.

Five minutes later, I was driving along the road on which Jack had lived for years. And, sure enough, there he was, out and about and heading straight toward me, only this time with a very noticeable limp that I hadn't seen before and coming from the direction of Saltaire village. I knew from the radio that Jack should be arrested for causing criminal damage but wasn't quite prepared for what I was about to discover.

As he came nearer, it became obvious that Jack had a large wet bloodstain on his jeans. And the amount of blood was quite startling. It covered the lower half of his left buttock and went a good way down his thigh, increasing in size as we stood looking at it. I asked him about the injury and he was his usual forthright self. 'I've been stabbed up the fucking arse by that bastard Steve,' he said, before admitting that he had indeed been the man wielding the frying pan, while claiming that he had been using it in self-defence.

Although it was Friday night, Jack was still clad in the clothes he wore as a welder: steel-toecapped leather boots, dirty jeans and a lumberjack-style checked shirt. It was obvious, therefore, that he had been drinking since finishing work seven hours ago. Yet even by his drunken standards, all of this seemed rather unusual.

I contacted Karl - who was still at the house in Saltaire - by radio, reporting the stab wound and telling him who Jack had said was responsible. This account was backed up by a search of the house, where a blood-stained carving knife was recovered from the kitchen sink. In no time at all, Steve too was arrested, in his case on suspicion of wounding. Both men were then conveyed to the cells at Bradford Bridewell in separate vehicles.

Karl and his prisoner arrived five minutes before us and went straight through the waiting area so that the formal booking-in process could be completed. Minutes later, Jack and I entered the waiting area. I could hear the voices of Karl and Steve, already at the charge desk next door with the custody sergeant. Karl gave him the details of the arrest and Steve's personal details. This wasn't the first time that our prisoners had been arrested, in fact they were both old hands, so they knew exactly what to expect. Jack heard his mate in the next room and shouted: 'Steve, it's me, Jack! Tell em nowt!'

To which Steve replied: 'No. Don't you say owt either.'

If nothing else, you had to admire the loyalty of two men who, only thirty minutes earlier, had been trying to kill one another. And then: 'If you get out first, wait for me outside and we'll share a taxi home.'

I didn't know what Steve said to the custody sergeant but ten minutes or so later it was our turn to go through to the charge desk. Once there, I outlined the reason for the arrest and pointed out that Jack had been stabbed in the left buttock, a potentially serious injury. The custody officer has a duty of care for all prisoners and will usually send a case such as this one straight to hospital with the arresting officer as an escort. But first he wanted to verify what I had told him and asked Jack to drop his jeans.

'You can get stuffed,' came the response. 'I haven't got a wound and even if I had I wouldn't be showing it to you. You're not looking up my arse, you dirty old git.'

Of course, this gave the custody sergeant something of a dilemma. A prisoner cannot be given medical attention if he doesn't want it. Despite his limp and the fact that Jack still had fresh blood running down his trouser leg, we couldn't forcibly examine the wound. One further problem was that Jack had been arrested on suspicion of breaking Steve's windows but the man in question had apparently told the custody officer that he had broken his own windows and it had been nothing to do with Jack.

As a result, both prisoners waited in the cells while we discussed this bizarre case. We had two crimes: a potentially serious wounding with a knife and criminal damage to windows. We also had two prisoners. What we didn't have was complainants and, to make matters worse, both men insisted that the other was completely innocent, thereby providing their pal with an alibi. The custody sergeant came to the inevitable conclusion that there was no possibility of a conviction and, within an hour, both were released without charge and last seen tottering away from the station with their arms draped around each other's shoulders, Jack still limping badly.

Later, the full story emerged from a female who had been in the house, Steve's girlfriend, whom Jack had tried to chat up in full view of her other half. Taking exception to this, Steve lost his temper and chased Jack round the room with the carving knife. As the terrified valentino raced through the kitchen he picked up a frying pan to defend himself but was stabbed in the backside before he could get outside and exact his retribution on the ground floor windows.

What a result. No complaint, no crime, no paperwork. Two prisoners, several broken windows and one stabbing up the arse. Now that's what I call a good night's work.

WOOD END estate didn't really belong in my image of Shipley; a small residential town about five miles north of Bradford, on the edge of Baildon Moor and Shipley Glen. Yet the grand houses lining the main roads, together with the lovely parks and the wide open spaces, hid a dark side that could be missed by the casual observer. The council estates in the Windhill area, for example, were every bit as rundown and deprived as any in the much larger cities of Bradford and Leeds; the only difference was size.

This had come as something of a shock on my transfer there from Manningham. And Wood End, in particular, was regarded as home to the unemployed, the drug dealers and the criminals. That wasn't absolutely the case, it never is, but decent tenants were few and far between. Its blocks of flats were dirty grey concrete structures; four storeys high with central staircase access to the upper floors. This staircase, along with verandas running the length of the buildings, was used variously as a communal dustbin or outside toilet. The council had given up any attempt at maintenance. Only the very desperate would want to live in such conditions.

One night, approaching ten o'clock, I was about to finish my shift when the radio interrupted my plans with a message about a Wood End incident. A man had been set on fire before jumping or falling from a balcony. Otherwise, details were vague. The ambulance and fire brigade had also been requested, standard practice for such a report.

Minutes later, I arrived at the scene. Abandoning the police car on the corner, I ran over a grassed area to where a group of four or five people were crouched in a scrum. What they were gathered around was a white quilt that had been used to cover someone laid on the grass. As I approached, I heard a young female shouting hysterically: 'Stuart, Stuart, please wake up.' Upon slowly removing the quilt, I saw that the object of her attentions was a young man, laying on his right side, legs tucked up, in the foetal position. At first I thought Stuart was a black-skinned youth, but I was wrong. He was, in fact, white. Minutes earlier, he had been engulfed in flames.

From previous experience, I knew that even though the flames had been extinguished he might still be burning up inside. He needed water pouring over him immediately and I shouted at a neighbour who was watching from the open doorway of another flat to bring it. The ambulance and fire brigade had not yet arrived so the responsibility fell to me to decide what should be done next. Stuart's shirt had been completely burnt away, apart from the sleeves and collar. His jeans had also been badly damaged. So much so that only his legs, from the thighs down, were now clothed. Even though we were outside in the fresh air the smell from this poor young man was indescribable. The whole of his upper body was black and charred. Stuart didn't speak or move; it was difficult to tell if he was dead or alive. I held his wrist and tried to feel for a pulse but his burnt skin sheared off under my fingers. His melted skin stuck to mine and I dropped his wrist without knowing if he had a pulse or not.

A small crowd began to gather - females screaming when they saw the condition of Stuart, a few young men, some drunk but not wanting to miss out on something they could talk about tomorrow. And then, after what seemed an age, came the welcome sound of sirens, first the ambulance and then a fire engine. Their crews hurried over, an oxygen mask was put over Stuart's face and bottles of cold water were poured over his charred flesh. He was still alive - just, it seemed - but not moving. And once he had been put on a stretcher and carried off to the ambulance, I began to take witness details. Written statements could be obtained later. First, I needed to discover who Stuart was.

Remarkably, as the paramedics got to work in the back of the ambulance, Stuart himself began to shout in pain, often using abusive language. Even so, that was good to hear. Only a few minutes ago, I had thought that he would never make another noise. Maybe I had been wrong; he was going to survive after all. Perhaps he wasn't as badly burnt as he appeared and the blackness of his skin was the result of smoke rather than flames.

The ambulance crew set off to hospital and I was joined

by a fire investigation officer. We entered Stuart's flat on the second floor. It was sparsely furnished, with little more than a wooden rocking chair and single divan bed. There was no food in the cupboards and no carpets. It looked more like a camp site than a home. My first thought was that this may have been a suicide attempt, so I checked all the obvious places. But there wasn't any suicide note. Had this young man tried to take his own life or was it all some terrible accident?

Coming back out of the bedroom, I saw that the fire investigator was on his hands and knees in the living room. He lifted spent matches from cracks between the floorboards and had also found a strip of newspaper folded into a taper. It was about ten inches long, half of it charred where it had been pushed into the gas fire. On the floor at the side of the chair was an empty plastic bottle, laid on its side. Checking the label, I saw that it had contained white spirit. A blue plastic top was a couple of feet away. With a price of 79p stuck to the side, the bottle had been bought at the local grocery shop. This loosely termed living room had a large metal framed picture window - measuring about four-foot square - looking out onto the balcony. Alongside it was a matching door. The window was now completely smashed and the broken shards of glass were either on the floor of the flat or outside on the balcony.

I then spoke to the neighbours directly opposite who told me that, suddenly, they had seen a bright yellow flame erupt in Stuart's flat. And when it then began to move around the room, they realised it could only be a person on fire. The person in question either dived or fell through the glass window before landing on the balcony and getting back to his feet, engulfed in a fireball, with bright yellow flames bellowing from his upper body. He then tumbled over the front of the balcony and landed on the grass below. By the time his neighbours reached him the flames were just about extinguished, his clothing was mainly burnt away and no doubt all the white spirit had been consumed by the heat.

Soon, with the evidence from the scene and that of his neighbours, a likely sequence of events was established. Probably, Stuart had been sitting in his rocking chair and decided to take his own life. He had already returned from the corner shop with a bottle of white spirit and now poured it over his head trying, unsuccessfully, to ignite it with matches. When that didn't work, he turned on the gas fire instead and pushed the newspaper taper in. What happened next we will never know. Did he ignite the white spirit deliberately or did vapour take light from the heat? Either way, the result was the same; he was soon engulfed in flames.

Stuart's parents lived on the very same estate, not five minutes walk away. But until I knocked on their door they hadn't heard anything about any fire. They were both about fifty years of age and Stuart was the youngest of four children. Recently, they said, he had been depressed after splitting up with his girlfriend. He had also been unemployed since leaving school with little prospect of finding work. I didn't have the heart - or nerve - to tell them how badly injured their son appeared to be, so I took the easy way out, telling them they would need to go to hospital for an update on his condition.

Stuart hung on for five more days before his vital organs finally gave up the battle and he passed mercifully away. There was little doubt that he had taken his own life, depressed and living alone in that awful environment, in the most horrible way imaginable. Yet it would be another ten years before those flats reached a point where the council at last realised that they were not fit for human habitation and had them demolished.

A GENTLEMAN, aged about sixty-five, had been seen walking along the footpath beside the Leeds to Liverpool canal, near Saltaire. Turning off, he went into a tree-filled area known locally as Hirst Woods. Nothing particularly unusual about that, until the person making the call told us that the chap in question had a bed sheet slung over one shoulder which, apparently, contained a sizeable and heavy object. And most sinister of all, this object had the definite appearance of a dead body.

At first, the woman who witnessed this potentially macabre incident went home and thought about it for a couple of days, before finally deciding that maybe she had better call the police. An officer was duly dispatched who knew the area well and he began to search the woods, although it was generally agreed that he would be looking for a needle in a haystack. In any case, was this concern genuine or was it just some sort of crank call?

Half an hour into the search, the officer had a stroke of good fortune, happening upon what appeared to be fresh digging deep within the woods. The soil had recently been disturbed and was slightly raised above the surrounding ground; all the hallmarks of a grave.

Upon the news, the police system swung into action. Senior detectives were sent to the location. Crime scene tape was wrapped around the trunks of convenient trees in order to prevent contamination. Uniformed officers diverted the public to preserve evidence. Officers were dispatched from the Task Force whose job would be to dig up the grave so that crime officers could go about their business.

Soon, word would be out and reporters from the radio, newspapers and television would be swarming all over the place. They even have their own helicopters these days; we would have little chance of preserving the scene. No doubt there would also be numerous kids off the nearby council estate hoping for the grisly sight of an exhumed body.

Together with a fellow officer named Eddie Gillard, I was one of the uniformed officers guarding the scene. Task Force officers, meanwhile, arrived in their overalls, spades at the ready. They got to work, carefully removing the loose earth and setting it to one side. We watched with morbid curiosity as the grave was taken painstakingly apart. Then, after around half an hour, there were shouts from the diggers and activity around the grave suddenly increased.

They had found something. We couldn't see what it was as we were too far away, but we could see the look of surprise on the faces of the men doing the digging. Yet suddenly the mood lightened. We were told that we no longer had to guard the crime scene and were invited to see what the grave contained. It was indeed a body, albeit not quite the type of body expected.

In fact, it wasn't a person at all. It was a large and very old golden labrador retriever. That was a relief. Well, at least it was to me. The senior officer looked a bit disappointed. He wasn't going to have his two minutes of fame on *News at Ten* tonight after all. It all made sense, really. Hirst Woods is a favourite place for dog walkers and no doubt this burial place was on the poor mutt's favourite walk. I looked around and it was indeed a very fitting place for a beloved pet to be laid to rest. It was autumn and the colours of the trees were beautiful. This was a secluded part of the woodland, so it had a feeling of being peaceful and tranquil. It would also enable the dog's owner to return to this location with fond memories of many years of happy companionship.

The senior officer, having lost out on his moment of glory, was not prepared to show such compassion however.

His big moment had been stolen from him and he declared that the dog should be removed from the grave and disposed of. As this was no longer a crime scene, he selected Eddie and I to transport the corpse back to Bingley police station. The following day, the council would collect the deceased hound and dispose of it in the incinerator.

The Task Force had done its job and wanted to return to Wakefield. They were not interested in filling in the grave they had just excavated. It was therefore left open for all to see. Eddie and I hauled the dog out and carried it away on a plastic sheet. It was a slow half-mile walk back to the car before we could place it in the boot and transport it to Bingley.

I often wondered about that dog owner. It was a heavy dog and he had gone to a great deal of trouble to bury it in that particular spot. What would he think when he returned there only to find an open grave? Maybe he would think that some ghouls had stolen the body of his one-time companion.

There is no doubt that the senior officer in charge was only following the rules that govern such incidents, but I couldn't help but think that on this occasion a little common sense and compassion might have been in order. The dog could have been reburied and the owner would never have been aware of what had just taken place.

# 12

*

# Racial Harmony

THE brand new Vauxhall Astra patrol car had been delivered to Keighley police station that very morning. After spending the past week at a garage in Bradford, having its roof lights, radio and insignia fitted, here it finally was, waiting for me to drive it. I deserved that pleasure, having put up with the old wreck it replaced for the past two years, with its tired engine, knackered gearbox, aversion to second gear and the body odour and smoking habits of dozens of former drivers.

So I had a spring in my step as I picked up the keys from the sergeant. 'Make sure you look after it,' he said. 'It's only got forty-eight miles on the clock.' Well, that gave the game away didn't it? The bugger had already been out in it before I started my shift. I walked back to the locker room to collect my kit. If the radio was quiet I was going for a test drive.

Passing the enquiry desk, though, I was stopped by a middle-aged Asian gentleman. 'Excuse me, officer,' he said, with a worried expression on his face. 'I am here to report that my thirteen-year-old daughter has run away from home, but I parked my car around the back of the station and a hit and run driver has just crashed into it.'

This, then, would mean filling in two reports. And, as usual in missing persons cases, one of them - the MISPER - would involve my searching his house, to make sure that the girl wasn't just hiding somewhere. 'Why don't we do it this way, Mr Khan,' I suggested. 'You go home and find all your driving documents and I'll come over in about ten minutes to search your house and take both reports at once.' He seemed happy enough with that idea and, as for me, at least it would give me a chance to drive my new car, if only for a short distance. 'Thank you, officer,' he said. 'That is very kind of you.'

What a nice man, I thought, as I loaded my kit onto the back seat of the new car and got ready to go. Climbing into the driver's seat, I sat back to inspect all the instruments and, after turning the ignition, listened contentedly to the quiet rumble of the engine. It had that distinctive new car smell of plastic and carpets. The door pockets were empty and spotlessly clean. No fast food cartons or old newspapers stinking of fish and chips. A glove compartment containing only the manufacturer's handbook. No discarded plastic tubes for the breathalyzer machine. No half-used booklets of search forms or producer forms for motorists' documents. The vehicle was perfect, although I knew it wouldn't remain that way for long.

As it turned out, Mr Khan lived about halfway along Dalton Lane, an area that many years ago would have been a hive of heavy manufacturing industry. Nowadays, redundant factories and engineering workshops line both sides of the road. The Khan residence was a small terraced house in an enclave of four streets, right in the middle of mostly empty industrial buildings. His car was parked outside. A dent to his front nearside wing was clearly visible from his encounter with the hit and run driver. Noting that the frontage of each house was no greater than the length of a single car and that each already had a vehicle parked outside, I decided to park about fifty yards away on one of the adjoining terraced streets.

With my paperwork on a clipboard I got out of the car and carefully made sure that it was locked before walking away. However, I couldn't resist taking a quick glance back before I turned the corner onto Mr Khan's street; it looked really smart and shone like a brand new pin. I couldn't wait to take it out for a proper drive that evening. Maybe I would drive over the moors to Ilkley and then back into Keighley via the beautiful Wharfe valley.

Mr Khan answered the door and welcomed me into his tiny home. The front door led directly into the living room and he beckoned towards one of a pair of large settees that took up the two main walls. His welcome and hospitality was typical of Asian families of that generation. I was offered tea and asked whether I would like anything to eat. I accepted the milky tea but declined the food and we then got down to business.

The accident report was fairly straightforward. He only had a partial registration number, the offending vehicle had been a tatty red Nissan and his rather vague description of the driver indicated a white male aged about twenty. I filled out the report and took a brief statement, before moving on to the subject of his daughter. I could tell that although she had only been missing for one night, he was very concerned about her.

Part way through this report I heard a dull thud from the street outside, followed by a bit of a cheer. It sounded like teenagers messing about. I gave it no more thought and told Mr Khan that I would have to search the entire house prior to leaving. Having no objection to that, he led me through each room, including the attic, cellar and back-yard outbuilding. There was no sign of anyone and before I left I reassured him that his daughter's description would be circulated nationwide. Her relatives and friends would also be checked up on.

Stepping out into the evening sunshine, I reflected on what beautiful weather we were having, perfect for a drive to the more rural parts of our division. But then, after walking the fifty or so yards to the junction where I was parked, I saw it. Initially, it appeared that some joker had plonked a 'no parking' cone on the roof but it didn't take me long to realise that it was far worse than that. Every single window had been smashed, there wasn't one left intact. Fragments of glass were everywhere. Inside, there were piles of it on seats, the dashboard and rear parcel shelf, while glass completely covered the carpet. Outside, the road and pathway was covered too, crunching beneath my boots.

I was devastated and very angry. At the other end of the street, three lads were playing football. They must have done it, I thought, or at least know who did. I marched over to them, seriously contemplating murder.

'Do you know who's done that to my car?' I demanded.

'No, nowt to do with us. It was like that when we came out. Thought it must have been dumped there,' they said.

'What do you mean DUMPED? It's brand new today.'

The lads just shrugged their shoulders and carried on with their game. It was obvious they weren't responsible; they were far too calm. The culprits were probably long gone and in this sort of area I was never going to find them. Reluctantly I got onto the radio and told the control room what had happened. I said that my car was no longer drivable and that they would have to send a recovery truck out from the police garage at Bradford. In which case, I had about an hour to kill, so I went back to Mr Khan's house and told him my tale of woe. Needless to say we sat down and had another cup of tea, until I heard on the radio that the recovery truck was now around the corner.

I thanked Mr Khan and wandered back towards my car, this time a little less enthusiastically and feeling sorry for myself. I turned the corner and saw the orange flashing light. The driver was reversing an old Vauxhall Astra off the back so that he could replace it with my freshly bashed in new one. And, yes, the car in question was the very same one that I thought I had got rid of. More happily, Mr Khan's daughter was found and returned to her father within twenty-four hours.


IT was July 2001 and racial tension in the city of Bradford had been bubbling for months. Recently, over the border in Lancashire, there had been riots on the streets of Oldham and Burnley. Bradford's ethnic population was bigger than that of those two towns added together. There was a feeling that civil unrest was inevitable and every possibility that it would turn into a full blown riot. Nor would it be the first time. Racial tension was nothing new in Bradford. The scars of riots past could still be seen and felt.

Threatening to bring current matters to a head, both the Anti Nazi League and National Front had planned marches through the city centre at the very same time. As everyone held their breath, the Government, in the shape of Home Secretary David Blunkett, intervened. The National Front march would be banned, but the Anti Nazi League event could go ahead. Undeterred, young nationalist thugs continued to arrive as planned. By midday, large numbers of them had gathered in the city centre pubs. The flash point, when it occurred, came outside one of those public houses, when a white National Front supporter was stabbed by an

Asian youth. And the events sparked would change the culture and communities of the city for years to come.

Despite the bubbling tension in Bradford itself, out there on the outskirts I had enjoyed a leisurely morning. I'd done a spot of gardening and then sat with a cup of tea and read the *Yorkshire Post*. An article touched briefly on the planned activities of the National Front and Anti Nazi League but it was nothing of which I wasn't already aware. After a light lunch, I set off for work at Bingley police station, shouting to my wife as I left the house: 'See you just after ten, with a bit of luck.' As comments go, that was nothing more than wishful thinking. It was a mid-summer Saturday, the pubs would be heaving, and there was no chance of finishing before midnight. It might easily be two or three o'clock in the morning before my shift finally came to an end.

I arrived at work just before two in the afternoon, by which time there had already been numerous skirmishes and fist fights in Bradford city centre. Yet that was nothing compared to what would take place in the coming hours.

At first, there appeared to be no urgency, although I was told straight away by the sergeant that my duties for the day had now changed. I would no longer be driving a panda to various jobs in and around Bingley, typically attending reports of vehicle theft and burglaries for the first hour or so, before moving through kids causing a nuisance and minor road traffic incidents to fully-fledged pub fights later. On this particular Saturday, there was something else in store.

Today I would be part of a police support unit (PSU), a team of fully-trained officers equipped with riot equipment who can be deployed anywhere in the area to deal with large scale public disorder. Initially, we would be on stand-by, held in reserve, and only called into action if the front line officers were unable to cope. So we loaded our equipment into a van and set off on a steady drive towards Bradford police station, anticipating a day of inactivity and boredom there. From past experience I knew that the police force often over-reacts to situations of disorder, especially when race is an issue. I wrongly assumed that the same thing would happen today.

Given that my radio was tuned into the same frequency as the officers on the city streets, it soon became obvious that events were turning rather more serious. Increasingly, their transmissions began to sound a little frantic and a touch of panic could be heard in some voices. As the afternoon drew on, reports came in of a second stabbing and groups of youths - white and Asian - were engaged in running battles all over the city centre. Windows were being broken and, apparently, looting was taking place. Consequently, the police on the ground were, indeed, struggling to maintain law and order. It was time for the occupants of our van to don our own protective clothing and equipment. From a big blue canvas holdall I pulled out a stab vest, leg and arm protectors and flameproof overalls, and put them on. I shoved leather gloves and a flameproof balaclava into my pockets and got my NATO helmet and clear plastic riot shield in place. Now, I was ready for anything.

'Right, van up,' shouted our commander. 'We're going to Whetley Hill to replace PSUs on the front line. They are taking a right battering up there.'

As we were driven the short distance to the bottom of Whetley Hill, the mood of our little gang was light-hearted, almost jovial, the general consensus amongst my colleagues being that this was going to be much more exciting than mundane police work. The van was parked at the side of the road and we climbed out, whereupon the noise that hit us was deafening. Shouting and screaming erupted from a huge mob, while the police helicopter overhead filming the rioters only added to the din with its rotor blades.

We had been told that there were now about a thousand people rioting. And, for sure, a mass of bodies filled the full width of the road and pavements on either side. The mob stretched back, thirty, forty, maybe even fifty yards deep. It was a mass of heads and flailing arms, with bricks and other debris launched high into the air and aimed at the front row of police officers. We were still over a hundred yards behind that front line, but the incessant sound of battered riot shields was chilling.

On went my flameproof balaclava and Nato helmet. I left my visor in the open position, so I could see where I was going. My riot shield was hooked securely onto my left forearm and my right hand gripped the second handle.

'Right, lads,' came the order. 'Form pairs and fill in on the front line. We are beginning to take casualties and gaps are opening up.'

My own partner would be Stuart, a dependable and trusted bloke who I worked with every day. I knew he would watch my back, just as I would watch his. We made our way through hundreds of our fellow police officers into the war zone, as numerous casualties were dragged back to the waiting vans, ahead of being evacuated to hospital. Some were walking wounded, limping and helped by a single colleague. Others appeared to be unconscious and were dragged by at least two officers with an arm apiece, heels scraping along the floor behind. Everywhere, shields and helmets were abandoned like worn-out artillery shells.

I pulled down my visor, which immediately reduced my vision by about fifty per cent. It was badly scratched through years of use and I should have had the helmet replaced ages ago. That was something I would soon regret. The continual din rendered the radio completely useless and I knew that visual contact would be essential if there was any chance of Stuart and I remaining together.

## Out of the Blue

Walking on, it became apparent that a good number of our colleagues looked completely exhausted. It was a hot summer's day and many of them just weren't used to hard physical work under layer upon layer of protective clothing and equipment. Dehydration and heat exhaustion seemed to be causing as many casualties as the bricks and missiles. When we eventually approached the front line, it was static. No one moved, either forward of back. There were maybe forty officers in total, spread over a width of fifty yards and, sure enough, gaps were indeed starting to appear where injured officers had previously been stood. I stepped into one such gap and Stuart squeezed in alongside me, as the bombardment continued with never more than seconds between the bricks or stones smashing into our shields. I kept my head down and tucked it into my shoulders. Where possible, I tried to 'field' the missiles passing just over my head, so that they didn't hit the lines of officers behind us.

Soon, it was obvious that we were just holding our ground, nothing more, nothing less. And this went against all the training I had ever taken part in. Surely, we were supposed to move forward, weren't we? To deprive the rioters of ammunition and deploy 'snatch teams' intended to break through our own front line and take prisoners? Weren't we supposed to keep the rioters continuously on the move, to stop them getting organised and using us for target practice? It wasn't long before I was having serious doubts about the competency of our commanding officers.

In front of our line was a gap of no more than thirty yards between us and the leading group of rioters, no man's land territory in which neither side was prepared to tread. Over it, anything that could be picked up and hurled at the police had been thrown. Bricks, broken glass, lumps of concrete, paving stones, lengths of timber and even traffic cones littered the road surface. Meanwhile, our own front line had continued to be bolstered, shields raised in a transparent wall of plastic. Unfortunately, though, these were so-called intermediate shields, slightly over a metre in length and short enough to carry when chasing a rioter. Less usefully, they offered only limited protection against a barrage of missiles, hence so many casualties. Should you use them to protect your head or legs? They simply weren't long enough to do both.

As the bricks continued to rain down and increase in intensity whenever the rioters found a fresh source of ammunition, the ammunition got even more imaginative. Soon, roof slates were also being thrown, skimming through the air like frisbees for a dog, their sharp edges more than capable of slashing unprotected flesh. The rioters must have been demolishing outbuildings. Most often, these objects harmlessly struck a shield but, every few minutes, a brick or roofing slate would find its way over and smash into a helmet or unprotected shoulder.

In short, we had reached stalemate. A thousand rioters at the top of a hill were throwing everything at five hundred officers half way up it and we were no more than sitting targets. It put me in mind of the children's nursery rhyme, *The Grand Old Duke of York*. 'When we were only halfway up, we were neither up nor down.' At least the Grand Old Duke of York had ten thousand men.

I felt sure that we should charge up the hill, disperse our attackers and, if we caught any, beat the hell out of them. But our commanding officers didn't seem to have the nerve for any of that. We were told to hold our line and take the incoming missiles on the chin, so to speak. But then, after four hours of such treatment, events took another turn for the worse. As it began to get dark, the rioters had another trick; covering their faces to avoid identification. And that, together with the bad light, reduced visibility through my scratched visor even more. The police helicopter overhead illuminated the area but the high-powered lights reflected off each and every one of those scratches. I could no longer see the missiles before they hit me. The first thing I knew about them was when they hit either my shield or my body.

As darkness descended, five or six Asian 'community leaders' stepped into the no man's land. They could easily have been hit by the missiles still being thrown from behind them, so that was quite brave. Their presence had a calming effect and, for the next few minutes, the bricks stopped flying as these Asian men negotiated with police commanders. This brought a lull in the storm, and gave us time to collect our thoughts and grab some bottled water. But it also provided the rioters with more time to re-arm.

It soon became apparent that the negotiations had not worked. Both parties wanted the other side to withdraw peacefully, but neither was prepared to do so. Community leaders and police commanders then scurried back behind their respective front lines, aware that the battle was about to intensify. The masonry had been bad enough, but now it was accompanied by fire bombs, or molotov cocktails as they are known. These appalling weapons are usually made from milk bottles half-filled with petrol, with a rag stuffed in the neck as a wick. When that wick is lit and the bottle thrown, the glass shatters on impact and petrol vapour is ignited, resulting in an immediate fireball. Part of my riot training had involved fire bombs, but that was in daylight and a controlled environment. There was always an officer standing by with a fire extinguisher in case anything went wrong. This was going to be very different.

At least there was one consolation. At night, the petrol bombs could be seen falling out of a darkened sky, which gave you a fighting chance to get out of the way. Before long, the bombs were hurtling over every couple of minutes and the bricks and roof slate bombardment continued too. A petrol bomb struck a riot shield about three yards to my left and spat fire in every direction. Instantly, that opened a gap in the line as three men jumped back, briefly alight, before banging their burning shields hard on the ground. They had been well trained. The burning petrol fell to earth and the stamping officers could extinguish the fire with their boots.

Shortly afterwards, another petrol bomb flew through the air, this time heading for me. Thankfully, it was a little too high and I was able to duck down and watch it pass over my head before it smashed on the ground behind me. The smell of petrol was intense and I could feel the heat on the backs of my legs as the officers there dealt with the flames.

Given that they were only thirty yards away, surely we were close enough to sprint forward and grab our assailants, arrest them and hand out the punishment they deserved? I for one would have gladly risked injury for an opportunity to get my hands on a fire bomber. But although we waited for such an instruction, it never came. We just continued to stand in line and take a hammering. The rioters, on the other hand, had licence to throw whatever they liked. If they wanted to throw bricks at us, go ahead. If they wanted to attack us with petrol bombs, carry on, that's quite alright. We police would just stand there and take it.

Another rag was ignited in another fire bomb; intended to be coming our way. Yet the outcome on this occasion was different. The wick was lit, followed by a flare of light. An arm arched backwards to gain momentum for the throw but then...disaster. The bomber had leant too far back and the burning rag fell out. Suddenly, the arm that had meant to hurl the bottle in our direction was engulfed in flames. That led to the bottle itself being dropped and smashing into pieces, allowing the petrol to ignite and set fire to still more of the rioters. Panic broke out as they tried to flee the flames.

The youth responsible for this turn of events ran around in circles with his right arm on fire and not knowing what to do. His clear distress was met by a big cheer from the line of police officers and I was happy to join in the celebration. It was a moment of laughter, a bit of light relief, and definitely an own goal by the opposition.

Then, up ahead, a gap opened in the lines of rioters. A white car appeared, old, battered and most probably stolen. Its doors were wide open and someone was messing around in the driver's side footwell. The bricks and firebombs still flew but I tried to ignore them and keep my concentration on the car. I thought I knew what they were planning and suddenly felt very vulnerable.

Sure enough, a group of the rioters got behind this car and began pushing it towards us. Its engine was racing; they had wedged a stick onto the accelerator pedal and rammed it into gear. That meant the car was heading straight for us and gaining speed as it careered down the steep hill. Now it was our turn to panic, as five or six of us all tried to jump backwards to get out of the way. A plastic riot shield offers little protection against a runaway car.

Unfortunately, we all had the very same idea at the very same time. As a result, we fell over one another, stumbling, trying to stay balanced; everyone desperate not to fall down and be run over. I couldn't get out of the way quickly enough, though, and the passenger side of the car smashed into my shield. I extended both arms with as much force as I could muster and was shoved backwards and away from its forward trajectory. The vehicle easily penetrated our front line but there were hundreds of officers behind us and, thankfully, the steering lock clicked on. After which, the car turned sharply left and lost its momentum as it collided with a building.

Now that our defences had been breached, the rioters

tried to seize the initiative. Dozens of them surged forward, armed with bricks and stones. I turned to face them and all of a sudden felt a heavy blow to the top of my shield. My left arm snapped back and the shield was rammed forcefully into my chest. The blow knocked me backwards and I stumbled for a few paces. Then I felt a tremendous whack to my head. I never saw it coming but a rioter had thrown a large stone into my helmet from a distance of no more than three yards. My head felt as if it had been hammered into my neck. I was staggering and disorientated when I heard a familiar voice. 'Dave, Dave, stand up,' it said. 'Don't fall down now.' It was Stuart, who had his arm around my back and was holding me upright, otherwise my knees would have buckled.

We moved back to the front and my head was spinning. A moment later, my eyes cleared and I saw that the top corner of my shield had gone. About a quarter of the shield was missing, jagged shards of plastic pointed up into the night sky. It must have caused by that first heavy blow. Quite obviously, some of these rioters were quite prepared to kill a police officer, and perhaps one of us.

We were still there well after midnight and hadn't moved forward for hours. As for police casualties, there were dozens and dozens. I saw Paul - a big powerful climbing friend of mine - go down, but I didn't see what hit him. It later transpired that a rioter approached him brandishing a six-foot steel scaffolding pole, held in the manner of a giant baseball bat. The rioter had swung the pole with great force and purposely aimed at Paul's legs rather than his riot shield. In any case, the effect was astonishing; my mate couldn't have hit the ground any quicker if he had been shot. His legs were smashed backwards so violently that his head had crashed onto the tarmac. He dropped his shield too and got to his hands and knees in a crawling position.

Stuart and I went to help him. We picked him up and moved away from danger. Understandably, Paul was confused. He lifted his visor and said: 'I can't see, I can't see.' His helmet and flameproof balaclava had been forced over his eyes. Stuart put his fingers inside Paul's helmet and pushed the balaclava back up his forehead. He was now able to see but still had a potentially serious head injury. We escorted him back through the ranks of other officers and arranged for one of the vans to take him to hospital.

Having done so, we took the opportunity to grab a drink of bottled water from the van. We hadn't had anything to eat now for over twelve hours and even the water was in short supply. Then, we walked back through the ranks of officers, making our way to the front line and re-joined our PSU serial, now depleted in number by at least a third. As we re-joined the line, a whispered message was passed along it: 'The assistant chief constable has authorised baton rounds.'

At last, baton rounds; what most people would refer to as rubber bullets. Great news. Something finally seemed to be happening. This will show the bastards. Let's give them some of their own medicine. The rioters had been trying to cause us serious injury, perhaps even death. At that moment I wanted revenge. Among the police, there was a buzz of excitement, a mood of optimism in the air. A few minutes later we got an update: 'The firearms teams would be deployed shortly.'

As we waited, the bricks and petrol bombs kept coming. We waited and waited. Just up the road, the Manningham Labour Club was attacked and burnt to the ground. A large prestigious BMW car dealership was attacked and looted before being set on fire and yet still we waited, taking all the punishment, total sitting ducks. In time, it emerged that our assistant chief constable had changed his mind. Baton rounds had never been used on the British mainland before and he obviously didn't fancy being the first senior officer to take that decision.

One of our commanders walked down our line trying to raise morale, but I had long since lost all patience with our senior officers. Seeing that my riot shield was broken, he said: 'Officer, that shield is useless. Drop back and get it replaced.' Oh yes, I thought. You can get stuffed. No one was going to want to swap shields and we didn't carry any spares. I ignored his instructions and turned my back. He would never be able to recognise me as he'd only seen me through my visor, so I had no intention of following his order.

By four-thirty in the morning the rioters had begun to dissipate. Only then did we start to move forward and push back the two or three hundred that remained. The damage they caused was horrendous. Burned-out cars and buildings lined the main roads and side streets. Dawn broke and, with that, the few remaining rioters melted into the shadows.

Eventually, when all the rioters had disappeared, we battered and bruised police officers trudged back down the hill on which we had been besieged all night. Surrounding roads would be closed to traffic for hours to come. There was an eerie silence; the only movement that of police vehicles. This mess would take some cleaning up. It was a scene of utter devastation but, right now, I was glad it would be somebody else's problem and not mine.

The van which had brought us now took us back to the Bradford Central police station. Upon our arrival, the car park was already full and even more vans were abandoned on nearby streets. I climbed out and waited for our sergeant, who had gone inside for a debrief. It was a lovely morning, with a clear blue sky and we were right in the heart of the city centre. So quiet and peaceful, completely at odds with the events of last night. I sat on the grass banking and looked around. For the first time I examined my helmet and saw that the top of it was smashed open like an eggshell; it had fared little better than my broken shield. The outer fibreglass was fractured, only the polystyrene inner padding had been protecting my head. Dozens of officers sat in their vans with the doors wide open or, like me, sprawled on the grass, some already asleep. On those faces still awake, there was a look of disbelief and shock. Tired faces. Exhausted, hungry and dehydrated faces. It was a scene similar, I imagine, to that which would follow any battle, weary foot soldiers grabbing a few minutes' hard-earned rest.

It was nearly six in the morning when we were finally dismissed, having spent sixteen hours on duty, much of it under attack. We were told to go home and rest. It is less than twenty miles to my home on the edge of the Yorkshire Dales but, once I got there, it felt like a million miles from the riots on the streets of Bradford. When I walked into our bedroom, I tried to be quiet but my wife heard me and woke up momentarily. 'Morning, are you alright,' she asked, half-asleep. 'Yes, I'm fine love. You go back to sleep.'

As I undressed and piled my filthy clothing on the floor, the smell of sweat, smoke and petrol was still in my nostrils. I was too tired to take a shower or even to brush my teeth. That would have to wait. For the first time, I saw myself in the mirror, upper arms and shoulders displaying huge black bruises. There were similar bruises on my lower legs and intense pain to the back of my neck, which felt similar to that of whiplash.

I climbed into bed and set my alarm clock to go off at twelve-thirty, only five-and-a-half hour's sleep after being awake for twenty-four hours. I would be back at work in only seven hours. It had been quite a night but I knew that I wouldn't have missed it for the world. I snuggled down under the duvet, content and finally safe. In less than two minutes, I would be sleeping the sleep of the dead.

# 13

\*

# Juliet Bravo

THE aftermath of the Bradford race riots saw an increase in police officers being diverted from their usual work to carry out public order patrols. In practice this meant that groups of officers in transit vans were sent to locations considered volatile and told to remain there until the perceived threat had ended. Much of this work was boring. Hour after hour in the back of a van or on standby in a police canteen. The idea was to prevent disorder by our presence rather than actually deal with it.

One Saturday night I was on just such a patrol in Halifax town centre. The crew consisted of an inspector, a sergeant, six PCs and me driving the van. We cruised around the town for a couple of hours without coming across any disorder. Most people were just having a pleasant night out and, while there was the usual amount of drunkenness, in good spirits.

Just after last orders we looked for somewhere to park up rather than drive round all night. This was partly because our inspector, a heavy smoker, had a habit of sneaking off to some back alley for a cigarette. The rest of us would remain with the van under the command of Sergeant Nowolski for lengthy periods.

Unfortunately Sgt Nowolski was about the most strait-laced person you could meet and did not share the sense of humour found so often in police officers. We soon realised that he'd just begun a relationship with a lady friend and they spent most of the time phoning or texting each other. He was obviously very much in love and constantly mocked by his colleagues as he spoke on his mobile to his sweetheart.

We had parked in George Square, where most of the pubs and clubs in Halifax are located. A police van parked on the precinct there does attract quite a lot of attention from the public, who are often under the influence of alcohol. We had been there for about half an hour when a group of women walked towards us. They'd had a bit to drink but that was only to be expected as they were out on a hen night. They weren't aggressive or offensive, just having fun.

As usual, our inspector had done his disappearing act and Sgt Nowolski was in the van whispering sweet nothings into the ear of his beloved. The rest of us were stood in pairs on the precinct. Sgt Nowolski was in the middle of the van's three front seats and therefore easily visible through the windscreen. He was engrossed, oblivious to the rest of us. We paid him little attention too, as we were busy observing the young ladies going in and out of the surrounding pubs and clubs.

Within this particular group of women was one dumpy little lady, around forty years old, who had clearly had one or two over the eight. She was very loud and jovial and easily the group's most vocal member. As she got closer, she shouted to her friends: 'Ey, watch this! I'm going to snog a policeman.'

The prospect of this didn't really fill me with joy or I'm

sure, any of my colleagues, but I didn't want to waste the opportunity. 'Hello, ladies,' I said. 'I bet you've never kissed a sergeant. Well, that's a sergeant there, sitting in our van.'

That was all the encouragement she needed. Bellowing that she was going to snog a sergeant, and goaded on by her pals, the lady pulled open the passenger door and began to climb inside. 'Give us a kiss,' she shrieked.

To say that Sgt Nowolski was taken by surprise would be an understatement. He had a look of absolute horror on his face. He clung onto his mobile and leaned away from this woman, so that his legs were in the passenger side but his upper body was on the driver's seat. He had the look of a condemned man and was clearly frightened to death. She, however, wasn't so easily put off. As her friends cheered and shouted encouragement, she was determined to have that kiss. And, to make matters worse, the love of Sgt Nowolski's life could hear every word.

'Get out! Get out of this van,' he shouted, as the rest of us looked on, laughing. 'But I want a kiss,' she replied, with a touch of aggression now in her voice, as she leaned over towards the unlucky sergeant while leaving her rather wide bottom sticking out into the street. Deciding that maybe she needed a little assistance, I placed my hands on her ample buttocks and gave them a hearty shove before slamming the door, a manoeuvre that left this pocket dynamo directly on top of Sgt Nowolski. Soon, she was slobbering all over him. 'Get off, get out,' he continued to yell in increasing desperation. 'I can't - they've locked me in,' she replied.

Eventually, the sergeant managed to free his legs from beneath his nemesis and escaped her clutches by scrambling out of the driver's door. That left the woman sprawled across the front seats with her skirt up around her waist. He stomped around the van to be greeted by seven policemen and a similar number of her friends, in stitches. He yanked open the passenger door and ordered the lovelorn lady out. He was beside himself, almost throwing a temper tantrum and jumping up and down in an uncontrollable rage. She, on the other hand, wasn't perturbed at all.

'I only wanted a bleeding kiss, you ugly old git.'

As the wannabe temptress tottered away laughing, Sgt Nowolski threatened that he was going to report us to the inspector. And, do you know what, he did, only to be told by his superior officer that our job was to interact with the public and that he should stop being such a miserable sod. I'm sure the inspector's only regret was that he hadn't been present at this romantic interaction himself.

BY 2004 Ted and Alice were already in their late-eighties and had been married for sixty-five years. Failing health was a problem but the elderly couple retained their independence and cared for each other in a small terraced house in Keighley. Daughter Mary was a regular visitor. She might cook them a meal or help with the cleaning, and she had her own house key. But as Mary let herself in one Monday afternoon, her worst nightmare was realised.

Road traffic officers aren't often sent to incidents such as these, but as all the other patrol officers were busy it was Barry and I who were dispatched to the scene. When we got there, Mary was standing outside the house waiting for our arrival. She was too frightened to go back inside on her own. She told us about a phonecall she had taken from her father. The call had made little sense, she said. He had been crying and saying over and over again that he was sorry, but he hadn't explained what he was sorry about.

Barry and I went into the house via a back door that led directly to the kitchen, only to be met with the terrifying scene that had greeted Mary only a few minutes before. In the corner of the room was a stainless steel sink, smeared in fresh blood. At the bottom of it was an equally bloody carving knife. Large drips of blood formed a trail leading from the sink to the doorway which, in turn, led through to the lounge; the only other room on the ground floor. Mary had got as far as this but been too afraid to go any further. It was at this point that she made a quick exit and telephoned for the emergency services.

My own heart was racing as I pushed open this lounge room door and stepped inside. Ted was directly in front of me, sitting on the settee but slumped back, motionless and silent, with his eyes slightly open. Speaking to him brought no response and his expression was glazed. I shook his arm and shouted 'Ted'; still there was no response. I felt for a pulse in his wrist. It was there but very faint, almost non-existent.

Barry had followed me in and it was he who went over to Alice. She was seated in a high-back chair, almost within touching distance of her husband. She too was in a bad way, semi-conscious and mumbling. Congealed blood covered her wrists and open wounds wept fresh blood onto the arms of the chair. The wounds were jagged and the flesh torn or ripped rather than cut. Alice appeared to be aware of our presence, but it was impossible to be sure.

Barry immediately ran back outside to collect the first aid kit from our car, while I updated the control room and informed the ambulance crew of the urgency. When Barry returned, we bandaged Alice's wrists and checked Ted for knife wounds. There didn't seem to be any. We couldn't work out why he was so poorly.

By this time Mary had summoned enough courage to re-enter the house and, despite her shock, was able to shed a little light on what had taken place. Her father had suffered for years with Parkinson's disease but, until recently, his wife had been able to look after him. This illness caused his hands to shake terribly, so much so that he was unable to feed himself or even hold a cup of tea. Then, about a month ago, Alice had suffered a stroke and was now unable to use her left arm or leg. She had to sleep downstairs on the settee and was no longer able to assist Ted.

The pieces of this sad jigsaw began to come together. The couple had been together for so long that they couldn't bear the thought of one of them dying while the other one lived. Instead, they decided to go together. Ted had taken on the responsibility and used a carving knife to slit Alice's wrists, but his shaking hands had stopped him from making clean cuts. His wife, meanwhile, sat calmly without complaint while he went about this last desperate act. She then watched as Ted's trembling hands pushed sleeping pills and painkillers into his own mouth. But Ted couldn't rest until he had telephoned his daughter. And when he did make that call, he couldn't find the right words to tell her what they had done.

Sitting together, Ted and Alice waited in silence for the end. This wasn't an act of violence but a love story that they both felt had reached its natural conclusion. These two people had been together for such a long time that neither of them feared what might come next. What did come next was Mary, closely followed by Barry and me. In turned out that we had arrived in the nick of time and the ambulance crew took Ted and Alice to the nearby hospital. Inevitably, the house had to be treated as a potential crime scene; there was a possibility that this may well end up as a suicide and murder investigation. The knife and empty bottles that had once contained Ted's tablets were seized as exhibits and the scene-of-crime photographers took pictures before the blood was cleaned up.

Belatedly, CID officers who, for some reason, hadn't been

available to attend when the call first came in soon turned up too, interested now that there was a potential murder to investigate. Barry and I took a statement from Mary and submitted a crime report in which Ted was named as the suspect and Alice the victim. However, I found it hard to believe that this was the most appropriate way of dealing with such a tragic event. It lacked any sort of compassion or human decency to accuse a man of Ted's age of being an attempted murderer.

More happily, despite spending many weeks in hospital, both Ted and Alice made a reasonable recovery from their shared ordeal and it was decided that they were physically unable to live by themselves, so together they moved into a local nursing home. Nor was it considered as being in the public interest to pursue any form of prosecution against Ted. It isn't always bad news.

SATURDAY night in Keighley town centre and we were fast approaching chucking-out time. A dry and mild evening, the FA Cup final had been played earlier in the day which, if anything, ensured an even greater consumption of alcohol in the town's nightclubs than usual.

On this particular night I was driving the road traffic car covering the division and had a bit of company; John was sitting alongside me in the passenger seat. A new recruit, the sergeant had put him with me because there were an odd number of officers at the briefing. Once, that would have meant us working separately, but inexperienced officers are no longer expected to walk by themselves, so he had the luxury of a car ride.

The first incident of the night was in Haworth, historical home of the famous Brontë sisters. During the daytime and particularly at weekends, Haworth's literary heritage can bring thousands of tourists flocking to the town. But they are usually day-trippers. On Saturday night, Haworth loses that appeal and reverts back to being just another part of a busy Keighley division. More Branwell Brontë than Charlotte.

A radio message directed John and I to an Asian restaurant on the main road. Two men had been in for a meal and, having eaten it, decided to run off without paying. Unfortunately, they'd drunk too much beer and were only capable of reaching the next street. As a result, a member of staff saw them as they entered a nearby taxi office. That was nice and convenient. As they sat down waiting for a taxi, our police car pulled up instead.

Gurdip, the restaurant employee, explained what had happened. The cost of the meal was £18.60, he said, but if the bill was paid he would agree not make an official complaint. Personally, I always resented being used as a debt collection agency for restaurants and sometimes taxis, but it is usually easier and quicker to get the miscreants to pay up rather than have to lock them away. Gurdip accompanied us inside the taxi office and pointed out the two men responsible. I decided immediately to lay my cards on the table.

'Right, lads,' I said. 'I understand you've been for a curry and then done a runner without paying.'

They looked at each other, at me and John and, finally, at Gurdip, before one of them worked up the courage to reply: 'We're not paying for it. It was crap. I wouldn't give that crap to my dog.'

I turned to Gurdip and asked: 'Did they eat the whole meal before they ran off?'

'Yes,' he replied. 'Every scrap and they never complained at the time. They waited until we weren't looking and then just run away.'

Having already seen and heard enough to make up my mind, I wasn't about to waste any more time on these two clowns. 'Listen, lads. You either pay up now or get locked up for the night in our cells. It's your choice. Which is it to be?'

They knew that they had been caught red-handed and that the choice I was offering wasn't really a choice at all. A few seconds of silence and then the same bloke reached into his back pocket and removed his wallet.

'Right,' he said. 'Looks like I'll have to pay. He's got no money and I'm not spending a night in them stinking cells. How much is it?'

Gurdip was quickly in with: '£18.60. And I don't want you back in our place again.'

A twenty pound note was duly offered which Gurdip gladly seized. No change was given and none requested, but I decided to keep that observation to myself. Just before we left, I turned to the taxi radio controller who had watched our exchange. 'Tell the driver who's taking these two fellas home to make sure that he get the money off them first. We wouldn't want them doing two runners in one night.'

How nice it would be if every job was as straightforward and easy as that. The complainants were happy. The runners were reasonably happy, because they hadn't been arrested. And we were happy, as the whole incident hadn't taken much more than ten minutes of our time. In this job, you don't get long to pat yourself on the back. Before we knew it, we were back down in the town centre on public order patrol. Then I would revert to road traffic duties, once the drunks were nicely tucked up in their beds.

As we drove along Keighley's main thoroughfare, North Street, it wasn't long before the first of many young people began to spill out of the nightclubs. And on the other side of the road staggered one likely candidate for 'Drunkard of the Evening'. In his late teens, twenty perhaps, or twenty-one at the most, he was tall, slim and gangly in appearance. In fact, so long were his legs that he didn't seem to have control of them. He reminded me of *Bambi*, the deer, from the Walt Disney cartoon of that name. As he headed towards Skipton Road, I slowed the car down to walking pace and stayed just behind him.

I know it's cruel to laugh at another's misfortune but I just love to watch a good drunk. Sometimes drunks can be so far gone they defy the laws of gravity, managing to remain upright despite logic demanding they fall in a heap. And this one was clearly going to be well worth watching. Wearing jeans in the fashionable style, that is, covering the bottom half of his backside with a good six inches of boxer shorts visible above the waistband, at first he made fairly good progress. He wasn't exactly putting one foot in front of the other, it was more that his steps were splayed out at an angle of forty-five degrees, but at least he was still on the pavement and moving in the right general direction. Then, for some reason, he decided to run.

Now, his running wasn't much faster than his walking; a gentle meandering trot would be a better description. But we could both see what was going to happen. With every step his jeans slid a little lower on his hips. A few more steps and they were past the point of no return. The lad himself, though, kept running, oblivious to the inevitable. And sure enough his jeans were soon below his crotch, yet he made no attempt to pull them back up. In another three steps his denims had fallen to his knees. After a fourth, they hit his ankles and then - whack - over he went, too drunk to put his arms out and break his fall, head first onto the ground. I pulled the car over to the side of the road, laughing so much I was unable to drive and, of course, keen to see what he would do next.

First, our well-oiled athlete rolled over onto his back and lifted himself into a sitting position. Then, he turned around and stared at the pavement, to see what mysterious object had tripped him up. Me, I could contain myself no longer. Winding down the window, I shouted across to him: 'Hey, you. It was your jeans.' He looked back, the first time he had seen us. No reply, just a blank stare. So I shouted again: 'It was your jeans. They fell down when you were running.' Only then did he notice that his legs were now bare and that his trousers were wrapped around his ankles.

Shuffling over to the wall of the nearest shop, he dragged himself back to his feet, very unsteadily. Then, with one hand clinging onto a door handle, he dragged at his pants until, just above the knees they got stuck. The jeans had a wide leather belt which was still fastened and therefore making it impossible to get the offending item of clothing over his hips. Not that he could work out why. In his present state of intoxication overcoming such a difficulty was quite beyond him. He mulled over his predicament for a minute and then made a decision; the jeans were as far up his legs as he was capable of getting them. Just beneath the crotch would have to do. So, he held onto the belt with one hand and steadied himself against the shop front with the other. Then, composing himself for a few seconds more, he gave us one final stare and staggered off along North Street heading for the taxi office. Hopefully he got home safely.

As for John and me, we drove away chuckling but I was soon in pensive mood. What did it say about me that I took such amusement out of watching someone behave in such a way? Was I some sort of latent voyeur, making covert study of drunken behaviour for my own enjoyment? I cast my mind back to when I first found such antics entertaining. It would have been in the early 1980s, when I was still in probation as a foot beat officer. I recall that I was standing in a recessed shop doorway on Commercial Street in Brighouse town centre. It was the early hours of the morning and the place was practically deserted. I saw him coming along the empty street; on the other side of the road and approaching from my right. As I was standing well back in the shadows he couldn't see me, although being so drunk he probably wouldn't have seen me if I'd been stood under a bright street lamp.

Anyway, this particular drunk was a short and stocky man, in his late-thirties. He wore crumpled trousers and a threequarter-length black leather jacket. I watched with interest as he weaved his way along the wide pavement heading for Bradford Road. I'd seen him before out and about, usually walking from one pub to the other, but I didn't know his name or anything about him, other than he liked to have a pint or two - sometimes six or seven.

Directly across the road was a sidestreet on a T-junction. Our man would need to cross this road if he was going to continue his progress along Commercial Street. You might think that crossing a sidestreet wouldn't be too much of a challenge when there's no traffic about, at three o'clock in the morning. But as I was about to witness, it can become an insurmountable obstacle if you've had enough to drink.

He slowed down, barely moving, and in doing so lost his forward momentum, coming to a stop in the middle of the path. He tried to set off again, lifting his right foot off the ground in an exaggerated step, but it was such a laboured movement that instead of stepping forward he lurched over to his right at an alarming angle and was suddenly off in that direction instead. Two, three steps to the right...left leg crossing in front of right...then behind it...sideways like a crab but with head pointed forward. Then came an almighty metallic crash as his shoulder smashed into the shutter of a greengrocer's shop window, sending reverberations around the town centre. Still, no harm done. Either to the drunk or the metal shutter.

I sniggered to myself, enjoying the floorshow, but there

was much more to come. He'd steadied himself now, legs splayed, with his back leaning into the protected window. Providing he didn't move, he was safe. Nobody could fall over from such a position. But he knew that he would have to move at some point. He couldn't remain propped up there until he was sober.

After what seemed an age, the drunkard made ready to move off once more. Worried that he might hear me, I had by now stopped laughing and tried to regain a little self control. He eased his feet back, directly beneath his body rather than out in front, and his balance seemed to be back in order. He pushed off the shutters with his shoulders, moving in the direction of the sidestreet. Three steps forward this time, but his legs were soon wobbly again. Arriving at the kerb edge, he came to a dead stop. Or at least his feet did. His upper body swayed back and forth as he glared down into the vast six-inch drop that would have to be negotiated if he was to reach his destination. Unsure and hesitant, he took a couple of minutes to pluck up his courage before finally committing himself to the challenge.

Meanwhile, I looked on in morbid fascination, willing him to step off the kerb. Go on, you can do it. Just try. If you don't, you'll be stood there all night. He must have sensed my encouragement. Bravely, he leaned forward but, to begin with, his feet wouldn't move and he looked as if he was about to land smack on his face. Then, at the last possible second, an inebriated message made its way from his brain to his legs and off he went. Walking in short quick steps, soon he was in the middle of the road, wobbling to the left and right as he went. And then, upon reaching the sidestreet, he paused to compose himself, breathing deeply now and mumbling incoherently. In a world of his own, it took all his powers of concentration to remain upright.

Now for the next phase of this self-inflicted obstacle race;

the task of stepping up the six-inch kerb opposite to get back onto the pavement and continue his journey. Resuming the same posture as before, feet about a shoulder's width apart, body swaying in a non-existent wind, he once again stared hard at the edge of the kerb. A step up this time, rather than down, should be easier surely?

I have studied drunks for years and can therefore say with some authority that maintaining a forward angle on the torso is the key to success. For some reason, if you lean forward but don't move your feet voluntarily, they suddenly start moving all by themselves. Maybe it's self-preservation. After all, if your feet don't move then you will very quickly land on your nose!

In any case, our hero had clearly made his mind up to go for it. And with three nimble steps he met the kerb head on. Tragically, however, he misjudged the height of the kerbstone and didn't quite get his left foot high enough. The toe of his shoe struck the concrete halfway up and over he tripped, heading straight for the plate glass window of a handily-placed furniture shop. He did manage to stamp his right foot down as a pivot, but he was going too fast to avoid the window and raised his hands to cushion the blow.

I too was expecting a disaster. As expected, he crashed into the glass but, thankfully, it held firm and he bounced back off. I breathed a huge sigh of relief. Bloody hell, that was close. I should arrest him for being drunk and incapable, I thought, reasoning that if I didn't, he might very well end up killing himself. But before I could get over the road to talk to him, I noticed that he was standing still again, peering into the shop at a dressing table with a large bevelled mirror on top of it. He was sizing himself up.

Only about three paces behind him now, I stayed silent as he took on the classical stance of a boxer. He raised both his hands and clenched his fists at about chin height, hunching his shoulders and tucking his chin into his neck. He then began to throw punches at his own reflection. A couple of left jabs, a right uppercut, then a haymaker with his left that nearly took him off his feet.

I bit my own tongue in trying to stay quiet; where was my video camera when I needed it? Jeremy Beadle or Harry Hill would pay a fortune for this. More seriously, I had to do something or else we would be here all night. Stepping forward, my reflection moved into the mirror beside his own. Suddenly, he stopped his shadow boxing and began to examine the mirror more intently, never thinking of looking back over his own shoulder, until I was unable to contain myself no longer. I cleared my throat and, for the first time, he swivelled around and realised that he had an audience.

At the sight of a uniformed police officer not three feet away, his mouth literally fell open as he lowered his fists and shoved them into his jacket pockets. 'I don't think that the boxing is a good idea, do you,' I said, but he didn't answer. 'Why don't you go home before you end up punching that other fella in the mirror and I end up having to lock you up?'

Still there was silence, but I'd had enough entertainment for one night and didn't really want to arrest him. 'Go on mate, get yourself home,' I said, 'and no more fighting, I'll be watching you all the way.' Bewildered and no doubt sobering up fast, he wandered quietly away while I stepped back into the shadows of the shop doorway to wait for whatever else might come along to amuse me.

# 14

\*

# Time for Reflection

MAYBE I was thinking too deeply about this accident. After all, that is just what it was, a road traffic accident, even if nowadays the official terminology is 'road traffic collision', a phrase considered less offensive to families of the deceased. For some reason, I could not stop imagining the moment before it happened. What had gone through the minds of the men involved? And why was I now trying to get inside their heads? I suppose it's just the way I am, and it does help to think in this way when you may be conducting interviews and following the investigation later.

The collision scene was on the A629 at Denholme, on the main road between Keighley and Halifax. I was working alongside Phil, my usual partner in the road traffic team at, without doubt, the most notorious road in the area for serious and fatal collisions. We had already been there for thirty minutes and it would be our job to try and work out what had happened and who, if anyone, was responsible.

An ambulance was in attendance but the deceased could

not be moved until the usual fifty or so photographs had been taken from every conceivable angle.

Among the protagonists at the scene was John, standing some distance from his skip lorry. It was still early days but first impressions were that it had been his driving that had caused this collision. In any case he was distraught, pacing back and forth, looking down at the ground and shaking his head in disbelief, not knowing which way to turn. There was only one other witness, a man who had been driving his car along the road as the impact occurred. He too was in shock but had seen everything and gave us our only independent account of events. This was a verbal account to begin with; later we would be able to help him to provide a written statement, once he'd had time to collect his thoughts.

The accident investigation branch (AIB) had also arrived; real specialists, more like scientists than police officers. Highly qualified, they made use of sophisticated equipment which allowed them to identify the slightest scuff or scratch mark on the road surface. From those marks they could prepare a plan of the collision scene. The AIB would also test the vehicles involved, ensuring they were in roadworthy condition, and decide whether the collision was due to some mechanical defect. The final part of their investigation was to reconstruct and determine the exact sequence of events.

Eventually, the time came for the deceased to be moved, by which point a small crowd had gathered, mostly the residents of nearby houses who had heard but not actually witnessed the collision. The A629 is a very busy road but fatal collisions have to be investigated thoroughly and so it was closed to all traffic. The Highways Department set up a diversion through nearby villages; it was eerily silent and would remain that way for several hours.

Our witness told us that he had seen the skip wagon pulling out of a driveway, before making a right turn across the path of the oncoming traffic. At the same time a motor cycle had been travelling in the opposite direction and been unable to stop in time. The motor cyclist had braked hard but the wheels locked and the bike slid from beneath him, causing bike and rider to part company. Both skidded across the road surface and smashed into the side of the skip wagon. The head of the motorcyclist struck the metal step under the driver's door, the impact sufficient to break his neck and cause near instant death.

As the skip lorry had pulled out into the main road in order to make a right turn; the suggestion was that John had failed to give way to the oncoming motor cycle. He therefore had to be arrested on suspicion of causing death by dangerous driving. I sat him in the police car while Phil delivered this news and there was dignified and quiet acceptance. He didn't reply. There would be no need for handcuffs or a police van to convey him in its cage back to the police station. He was devastated. Not because he had been arrested, but because his actions may have caused the death of another man. He asked if he could telephone his wife. The call was brief. He didn't tell her about the death, just that it was serious and that he was going to the police station.

Truck drivers are tough men. I don't know why but they often are. If the truck happens to be a skip wagon then that toughness is just about guaranteed; maybe they are the type who are attracted to that lifestyle. John looked the part. He may be in his fifties but he was still strong and fit, not tall, but with a broad and powerful build. He wasn't a man to be messed with but, right now, he was broken. He was taken to the station in the rear seat of another police car. There was no requirement for an escorting officer other than the driver. That wouldn't be needed, even if it was against normal police procedure.

We identified the owner of the motorcycle - a local man who lived only a few miles away - by its registration number. Another colleague visited the next of kin, the man's wife, to give her the devastating news and I didn't envy him that onerous task. The death seemed all the more personal when we discovered that the deceased had been a member of the emergency services; a fireman. He had been on his way home from Halifax after just finishing a shift there. It was a journey of around ten miles that would only take about twenty minutes. The road was well known to him and there was no suggestion that he was driving over the 50 mile per hour speed limit.

Even more tragically, it turned out that he also had a two-year-old daughter and that his wife was pregnant again. She was originally from Australia and the couple intended, in just a few weeks' time, to go live there and start a new life. Knowing all this made the man's death even more difficult to come to terms with. It was shattering for all concerned.

Back at the accident scene, the AIB got busy. The exact spot where the motorcycle first skidded was identified and scratch marks on the road surface indicated where it had toppled over before beginning its slide into the side of the lorry. In a restaging of events, that vehicle was reversed back into the driveway from where it had been delivering a skip and then driven out as fast as it could possibly travel, before making the right turn which replicated what John had been trying to do.

Three times this manoeuvre was carried out and each time it was carefully timed with a stopwatch. I then drove my police car towards the collision site from the same direction as that taken by the motorcycle. This allowed us to determine the how far ahead the rider would have been able to see along the road as he came around the bend. The final part of the scene investigation saw the carrying out of skid tests, which would determine how much grip was available before the bike's tyres lost their grip on the road surface.

The result of these tests was to take the investigation in a new and unexpected direction, as we established beyond doubt that neither driver had been at fault. The motorcycle was being ridden within the speed limit. He had just negotiated a left hand bend when he came around the corner and saw the skip wagon. It had already begun to pull out of the driveway on his nearside and was starting to make a right turn across his path. At the same time, the lorry driver saw the motorbike approaching but was already committed to pulling out at the same time as it emerged from the bend. That left John with no choice but to try and clear the road. The timing, which we recorded using the stopwatch, showed that this particular accident had been unavoidable. The motorcycle could not stop within the distance available to him, even though he was travelling within the speed limit. We also established that the skip wagon was incapable of completing its manoeuvre any quicker.

Later that evening we went back to the police station to carry out a formal interview with John. He didn't want a solicitor present, he just wanted to give an honest and open account. We explained the results of our findings which must have been a tremendous relief to him and, later, he was released without charge.

However, it was an incident that would no doubt stay in his mind forever. During the interview, John explained how he had not only seen the motorcycle coming, he had for a couple of seconds made eye to eye contact with its rider. He knew what was about to happen, as did the biker. Both men shared one fatal moment in time that would wreck the lives of so many.

NO one can carry on forever, not even yours truly. And so not long after the incident last described I decided to put the uniform away and bring the curtain down on twenty-six tough but eventful years.

Being a policeman is what they call being at the sharp end and, looking back, I feel quite proud of what I achieved. Nowadays, it is almost unheard of that someone will choose to police the streets at all hours of the day and night and then continue to work shifts for as long as I did. In fact, the opposite is more often the case. Many recruits hope for an office job or posting to a specialist department before they have even finished their two-year probationary period.

The period of my service - from 1981 until 2007 - saw three decades of unbelievable change, taking in riots, recessions, the invention of the internet and mobile phones, the development of DNA and so much more. In fact, there was so much change that it was difficult to keep up with it at times, but it has often been said that the police service merely reflects the society it serves. The job out there on the streets has never really differed. It is, was and probably always will be about the people you meet and how you deal with them. That is where the real and lasting memories are found. Whether it's friends, colleagues, criminals or the law abiding members of the public, there is always a story to tell.

Nor should the fact that many of these stories have more than their fair share of humour be any surprise, and much of it black humour too. For that is often how police officers amuse and support each other during times of incredible tragedy and sadness; a defence mechanism that is not always understood by those outside the force. The end, when it came though, was quite sudden.

Haydn, one of my colleagues in road traffic, had spent months planning his retirement. He knew down to the day and even the hour of the day when he would retire. It was the summer that the two of us had already arranged to go on a two-week wander on the coast to coast footpath across the width of northern England. Yet on the week of Haydn's retirement, I heard a rumour that I was about to be served with a witness court warning. That would mean I'd have to appear in court to give evidence when I should be midway through our walking holiday. The court case was for a very minor offence and my own evidence would have little significance on the final outcome. I had no intention of disrupting our longheld plans over such trivia.

So, I decided to short circuit the system and handed in my notice. I would retire on the day of my fiftieth birthday and, as I was already owed so much time, that left me with just two more days to work. To say the least, this was something of a shock to the system. I'd no idea that I would be able to retire quite so soon. I hadn't even told my wife; in fact I even considered not telling her at all, but knew I wouldn't get away with that for very long. My sergeant wasn't exactly jumping for joy either, but the decision had been made. My future, from now on, was going to be very different.

Mainly, I decided that after my retirement I would forget all about my days in the police and move on to other, less stressful activities. I intended to resume my former trade as a carpenter and joiner, for example, and was keen to travel extensively. Yet, unbeknown to me, it was while away on one of those travels that I was destined to face my biggest test of all.

# 15

**\***

# Living the Dream

WHAT a magnificent opportunity. Very few of us get the chance to follow our dream but, for me, everything was now in place.

By the time of my retirement from the police force I had long ago embarked upon a happy second marriage, my first having come to an end in the 1990s, mainly as a result of my shift patterns and a subsequent growing apart. There was no major falling out with my first wife but, as ever on such occasions, the break-up had been sad, painful and difficult, especially for our children. Eventually, though, homelife had settled back into contented normality.

Work-wise, I had one or two ongoing commitments in the building trade which needed completion before I could go anywhere. I had been working part-time on my days off, renovating two old cottages with the intention of renting them out and purchasing another for the same purpose. But, by April 2008, these projects were just about finished. I was fit, in good health and financially secure. The way was clear for the free spirit within me to travel to the far-flung corners of the earth. I couldn't wait to experience how other cultures lived without the trappings of material wealth. The world was my oyster. It seemed too good to be true.

I would still need to earn *some* money, of course, and so decided to divide my time between a part-time job of some sort and hitting the road. And, in that latter department, it didn't take me long to get myself organised. Soon, I had four holidays planned. First, I would walk the West Highland Way footpath with my former police friend, Haydn. Then I would spend a week in a log cabin in Perthshire with my lovely wife, Julie, and go walking in the mountains with our pet dog. By contrast, my third holiday was set to be solitary; I intended to cycle from Lands End to John O'Groats. And my final adventure of the year was to be with my son, Danny, the most adventurous expedition of all. We would go trekking and white water rafting in the Himalayan mountains of Nepal.

Once all that was done it would be November; time to return home and start filling in my travel diary for 2009. To some extent I realised that this might be seen as a rather selfish lifestyle, but I knew it was only for a limited number of years. In time, I would be too old to endure such physical hardship. And anyway, I felt I had earned the right to put myself first, having worked a sixty hour week for the past thirty-five years.

On the subject of retirement, I had often felt out of step with my former police friends and colleagues. Over the years, I listened with amusement as they talked about their own forthcoming plans. There would be a big party, lots of booze and speeches, and then a 'holiday of a lifetime', maybe a cruise with their long-suffering better half or an expensive hotel in Rome, the Caribbean or Hawaii. This was to be their reward, but it wasn't what I wanted. I was still hankering after thrills and excitement, some of it with Julie and Dan, but much of it unaccompanied.

Halfway through my first big year of travel, in August 2008, after having already taken the first two holidays with Haydn and Julie, I set off for the Outer Hebrides. Why the Outer Hebrides? Well, my original idea to cycle from Lands End to John O'Groats had brought nothing but frustration. I had been hoping to stick to quiet country roads and stay in Youth Hostels on route; however I soon discovered that England's Youth Hostels, particularly in Cornwall and Devon, tend to be located on main roads or near to seaside resorts. I didn't relish the prospect of cycling along busy roads with trucks thundering past. Also, getting myself and the bike to Lands End and then back from John O'Groats turned out to be far more complicated than I thought. The most logical way would have been via rail, but the initial journey south would involve four different trains, with three different trains needed on the way back. Furthermore, the bike had to be booked onto each individual train in advance, yet it would still be at the discretion of the guard as to whether he would allow it on board. All in all, a great deal of hassle, so I began to look for an alternative.

I found it in north west Scotland, a region already well known to me after around thirty years of climbing holidays there. It had good roads, very little traffic and plenty of accommodation available. I did, however, want to try somewhere unfamiliar and the Western Isles of the Inner and Outer Hebrides were the ideal solution. Julie and I had spent part of our honeymoon in the town of Oban on Scotland's west coast; so I knew it was from there that ferries sailed to all the Hebridean Islands. It would make an ideal port of departure.

Before long, a new touring bike had been purchased and fitted with four large panniers to carry all the camping equipment, together with food, a stove and all my clothing. Fully-laden, the bike was extremely heavy, in excess of one hundred pounds, but it carried everything I needed for two weeks' touring. I intended to be entirely independent and only stay in hostels if it was raining. That way I could decide whether I wanted to cycle any distance between twenty and sixty miles a day depending upon the conditions and my own energy levels.

The notion of such complete independence was highly appealing to me. Like most people, I had lived in a world where the clock and calendar dictated everything I did and for how long. The chance to escape those restrictions, even if only for a couple of weeks, seemed heavenly. My wristwatch would serve only one purpose; it would enable me to get to the ferry terminals on time. From now on, my day would be determined by the rising and setting of the sun.


ON August 8 2008, I packed my bike and luggage into the back of my estate car and left on a trouble-free overnight drive to Oban, just as darkness was falling. Once there, I would purchase an eight-day ticket for unlimited use of the Highlands ferry service and the car would be temporarily abandoned. I couldn't wait to actually get on the bike.

Now, I have always been a dinosaur with regard to new technology. I can just about cope with a mobile phone but I would be completely lost if I tried to send a text message, it is a skill that has simply passed me by. I also have a fondness for both sending and receiving hand-written letters. They can be read over and over again, and there is something old-fashioned and romantic about this form of communication, particularly if the person you are writing to is your wife. I had warned Julie that this was to be my intended form of communication and that she should not expect many phone calls. I also told her that my mobile would be switched off and would only be used in the event of an emergency.

What follows is an exact copy of the first letter I sent to Julie from Scotland. It would be the last letter she received from me for a very considerable time.

*Sunday 10 August*

Hello darling, hope you are all OK. I sent you a postcard yesterday from Lochmaddy in North Uist, but as there's no Sunday post you will probably get it on the same day as this.

The journey up to Oban was straightforward and I found a long-stay car park going down the hill into Oban. There were already plenty of cars there and it was floodlit, so I think the car will be as safe there as anywhere. I managed to sleep on the ferry for a couple of hours when going to Lochboisdale and it rained heavily for most of the journey.

On arriving at Lochboisdale the rain had stopped and for the first one-and-a-half hours it was dry, with empty roads and a good tail wind to push me along. There was a range of mountains to my right all along this road, but low cloud obscured the view and I was never able to see the top of the peaks. It then started raining and I got soaked, so I carried on riding rather than camp in the wet. I went over the causeway which separates the islands of South Uist and North Uist and finished my day at Lochmaddy at about 5pm. I had covered forty-four miles in about three-and-a-half hours, so I was pleased with that.

I managed to get a bed in an outdoor pursuits hostel. It was a bit hit-and-miss. Officially they were full, but I was told that if I could find an empty bed I could stay. Most of the other occupants were involved in sailing but I shared a room with a woman aged about thirty and a couple called Steve and Lisa. They were in their late fifties and have their own boat with them at the nearby harbour.

In the evening I walked into the village to post the cards

and then went into the pub. By coincidence, Steve and Lisa were already there so I enjoyed a couple of beers with them. I went to bed at about 10pm so that I could have an early start today.

My ferry sailed at 9am and, as I was about twelve miles from the port, I set off at 7.30. The road was absolutely deserted and went through lovely countryside so I really enjoyed the ride. The ferry had room for about one hundred cars but only one actually turned up. There was also a married couple on a tandem bike doing more or less the same route as I have planned. That was the full extent of the passenger list: five people, one car and two bikes.

The ferry crossing to Leverburgh in Harris was incredible. We had the best seats in the house on the front row of the passenger deck, rather like the captain of a ship. The map shows that the ferry zig-zags slightly when passing between the two Islands, but the journey itself was much more impressive. There are hundreds of rocky reefs between the two ports and the ferry is constantly changing direction, sometimes by up to ninety degrees to follow the deep water channel. From our seats I saw that, at times, we seemed to be heading on a collision course with the rocks, until the ferry went past a marker buoy and completely changed direction.

The ferry docked at 10am and I started to cycle round the west coast of south Harris. The weather was fair with a little sunshine but mainly cloudy. This part of the Hebrides is truly spectacular. There are beaches where the sand is almost white and the sea appears turquoise. Inland, the mountains are shrouded in low cloud and I could have stopped at almost every bay to take photographs. I took a couple of Taransay for you and also of a house which I think was featured on *Grand Designs*.

After about fifteen miles following the coast, the road started climbing up over a mountain pass which seemed to go on forever, but it provided fantastic views from the top. I then free-wheeled down the mountain road to Tarbert where I am now. I arrived here at twelve noon but have already covered thirty-four miles (including the mountain pass) so I'm going to have a lazy afternoon.

I called at the bunkhouse in Tarbert but they were full. The owner pointed over the wall to a patch of grass where he said people occasionally camped. This is a picnic area with tables and benches; twenty yards from the harbour and a hundred yards from the ferry terminal. A young French couple have come and pitched their tent next to mine but, apart from them, I have the place to myself. I cooked some dinner before starting to write this letter and it has just begun raining. At least that should get rid of the midges.

I'm changing my plans for tomorrow. I had intended to cycle up to Stornoway and then ride around in a big circle before returning here to Tarbert. That would be a distance of around one hundred miles to get back to where I started from, so I have decided to get the 7.30am ferry to Uig on Skye instead. This will save me a couple of days, so when I get back to Oban I may drive down the Mull of Kintyre and then take my bike on the ferry to the Isle of Arran. I think that may be a better proposition

I have tried to ring you but there is no signal whatsoever. If it stops raining I will walk into town and post this letter and try to phone. If not I will try from Skye.

Love you darling

Dave.

PS. The bike is fantastic!

THE weather did indeed change and, later that evening, I walked to the Harris Hotel in Tarbert, where I spent a pleasant couple of hours sampling the local ale and reading the memorabilia on the walls from the TV series *Castaway*.

Apparently this was the pub where a group of the original 'castaways' had stayed when they could no longer cope with life on the deserted island of Taransay. It had clearly attracted a great deal of local and national interest at the time. There were framed newspaper cuttings from just about every national newspaper.

By ten o'clock I was back at my tent and climbing into my sleeping bag. Unable to sleep, I began to look back over the last two days. Already I had seen so much and was looking forward enormously to the rest of the trip. As I had indicated in the letter, the following day I planned to cycle from the port of Uig at the northern end of Skye right down the length of the island, before taking the ferry to Mallaig on the Scottish mainland. I would then cycle due south through the Ardnamurchan peninsular before taking the ferry to the Isle of Mull. After cycling around the island it would then be back to Oban where I would collect my car and drive down the Mull of Kintyre. Once there, I would again leave the car and finish off my adventure by taking a ferry to the Isle of Arran and cycling around the entire island.

It was still early days but this growing sense of freedom and independence was so heady that I began to think it could become less of a holiday and more an entire way of life. Other possible trips crowded my brain. Ireland might be one destination. I could take the ferry to Belfast and then cycle along the north coast to explore the Giant's Causeway before, if time allowed, cycling the full length of the west coast. A trip back along the banks of the River Shannon would make it a circular route. I dreamed of taking a ferry to Rotterdam and through the Low Countries to Denmark, where I could then explore the new series of bridges and islands that now link Denmark to Sweden across the Baltic. That would be one hell of a journey and another circle could be completed by cycling into Norway and taking a ferry from Bergen back to Newcastle. There was really nothing to stop me, as long as I had the motivation. I slept soundly that night and woke early for a quick breakfast before packing away the tent and loading up my bike.

The ferry from Tarbert to Uig took about ninety minutes. The mountains of Skye came into view long before we arrived at the port and rain clouds could be seen around the mountain tops. Somehow that did not surprise me. Every other time I had been to Skye it had been raining. My last visit to this island had been ten years earlier, with a climbing friend named Andy. We had gone with the specific purpose of completing the traverse of the mountain ridge of the Cullin Mountains. Our interest had been generated by a magazine article written by a famous mountain guide. He had described our planned route as the most difficult in the British Isles and potentially harder than the Matterhorn and Mont Blanc put together. He also stated that the chances of completing this route in poor weather, or without an earlier recce where supply drops could be left on the ridge, were highly unlikely.

Despite the rain and low cloud we did complete the route, in forty-eight long and exhausting hours. We carried all our own equipment and supplies and slept overnight in bivvy bags, high on the ridge. Though delighted with the outcome, I was disappointed that the rain had obscured the views. I'd climbed all the mountains but hadn't seen them or their panoramas from the top. The day after our success, we drove into the only community of any size, Portree, where I bought a coffee table book intended for tourists. At least this had good photographs of where we had just spent the last two days.

This holiday though was for cycling, not climbing. My plan was to travel straight through the island in one day, a journey of some fifty miles. I left the ferry terminal and began to cycle steadily south. A fine drizzle was falling and there was little new of interest for me as I already knew the island reasonably well. On and on I pedalled until, after around three hours, I approached the Sligachan Hotel, a place that held fond memories. It was here that Andy and I had camped during our climbing trip a decade before.

As the rain was by now falling heavier, I decided to make this grand old place a convenient lunch stop. Placing my bike under the eaves of the roof and out of the rain, I went inside. It had changed little in the last ten years. Soon, I was sitting down with a beer and a large steaming bowl of soup, into which I dipped a substantial wedge of home-baked bread while I looked round the room, reminiscing.

Several minutes later I found myself joined by another cyclist, a man who I had bumped into earlier on the ferry. Unlike yours truly, this chap was what I would consider a 'proper' cyclist, with a fully-equipped lightweight racing bike. I had assumed that he would be miles ahead of me by now because he had been travelling virtually luggage-free. He didn't want to be burdened with camping gear and had booked ahead at bed and breakfast establishments, a wise move given the worsening weather conditions. We finished our meals and he told me that he was now on his way; but as the rain continued to pour outside I was reluctant to leave so soon. Undeterred, off he went, after zipping up the bright yellow jacket that was visible through the pub window as he cycled away south, heading for the same ferry that was also to be my destination.

Me, I hung around for another ten minutes until, when there was still no sign of the rain stopping, I resigned myself to the fact that I was going to have to get wet. Reluctantly, I put on my gortex jacket and ambled outside, before climbing onto my bike and pedalling away. I estimated that it would take about another two or three hours to reach the port, ample time given that there was around five hours before the ferry sailed.

I had been cycling for about twenty minutes when, in the distance, I saw that same yellow jacket about a mile ahead. Again I was surprised. Surely, he would be out of sight by now. The bobbing yellow jacket popped up on the horizon periodically over the next ten to fifteen minutes and I was able to measure my progress as the gap changed between the pair of us. Secretly, I was rather pleased with myself. Given that my bike was so heavily-laden, I must be fitter than I had realised.

These would be my last conscious thoughts.

# 16

*

# A Timely Intervention

ANDREW is a consultant anaesthetist at Guy's Hospital, London. On this particular day, he was holidaying on the Isle of Skye with his family and on his way to one of the local tourist attractions. As he drove downhill, a long descent all the way to Sligachan, he moved patiently in a line of tourist traffic held up by a slow-moving vehicle at the head of the queue; none of whose drivers were going any faster than 45 mph. Along with the recently worsening rain, a strong wind had now also begun to blow. Approaching in the opposite direction, came a cyclist. Andrew, a keen cyclist himself, couldn't resist taking a look. He saw the heavy panniers and knew that, soon, the rider would be urging his bike uphill into the wind and blustery rain. On a day such as this, he felt sorry for the poor bloke.

And then, having glanced in his driver's door mirror, an image was reflected back at Andrew which filled him with dread. It was a car, a Renault Laguna, that only seconds before had been several cars behind. Now, it had pulled out again and was accelerating quickly, trying to overtake the entire line of traffic in an impossible manoeuvre. It rounded two of the cars and then a third, but Andrew knew that there was no way it could slip back into the queue in time. The Laguna was going to collide head on with the cyclist, there was no escape route for either. Andrew didn't see the collision, it was now some distance behind, but he heard a tremendous crash and knew instantly what had occurred.

Events had played out at frightening speed, only a second, Andrew calculated, between his sighting of the Laguna and the sound of the impact. Precisely one second earlier, the gap between the Laguna and the cyclist had been 110ft; now it was zero. That was the distance covered by the two on their collision course. The Laguna, at 60mph, moved directly into the path of a bicycle travelling at 15mph. That meant a closing speed of 75mph and... disaster.

The first point of impact was the Laguna's front bumper, which hit the front tyre of the cycle and deformed slightly to absorb some of the kinetic energy, as it is designed to do. At the same time as the front wheel of the bike buckled, it was pushed back with such force that its forks were distorted and the spindle bolts holding the wheel in place were sheared. All of this meant that the cycle came to an instant stop, but its unlucky rider did not. He was thrown forward with tremendous force; flying over the handlebars and colliding with the windscreen of the Laguna, which was still travelling at nearly 60mph. The impact was over in the blink of an eye but, for that cyclist wending his way through the beautiful Scottish Highlands, it all unfolded in slow motion.

As car and bike collided, my natural instincts took over. I raised my arms, the usual reaction when flying through the air, before the palms of my hands smashed into the car windscreen, punching two holes through the laminated glass. This particular style of glass is designed to deform rather than shatter; rendering it safer for the occupants of the car. Accordingly, the windscreen momentarily buckled at first, while I continued on my forward trajectory and the glass sliced deeply into the palms of both hands, across the base of all the fingers. But worse was to follow. As my hands continued their passage, the slicing action also continued. The flesh was cut away, taking with it blood vessels, tendons and nerves. These deep lacerations extended from the base of my fingers almost to my wrists.

Next, it was the turn of my head to strike the windscreen, not straight on, but at an awkward angle. This resulted in my neck twisting and three vertebrae near the top of my spine were broken. The force of the impact split my cyclist's helmet down the middle, but somehow it remained attached to my head. Still the agony wasn't over. The kinetic energy of two moving objects was not yet spent, as cyclist and Laguna were absorbed deep into one another, almost merging into a single horrifying entity. My head smashed a large indentation in the windscreen, wrenching the bonding adhesive between the edges of the screen and the bodywork of the car apart and leaving the windscreen crumpled inside. For me, that meant there was no longer anything in place to stop my own headlong progress into the vehicle. Instantaneously, my body twisted around, led by my left knee and thigh, which smashed into the leading edge of the car roof. Without a windscreen in place, this was now a jagged metal edge, as deadly and sharp as the blade of any knife. This particular moment of impact fractured my femur in four places and ripped away yet more flesh and muscle.

And still my forward momentum continued through the longest second - no, *less* than a second - of my life. My legs were thrown upwards and over the roof of the car, dragging my upper body with them. Now I was no longer moving forwards but upwards, spat out and ejected up and over the car roof in flight, resulting in yet more injuries; five broken ribs and a punctured lung before, finally, coming to rest with a thud and a splash in a flooded peat bog at the side of the road, as mangled car and cyclist rapidly parted company.

Mercifully, by the time I hit the deck I was unconscious. Less mercifully, I was underwater and no longer breathing. The cold water had caused my blood vessels to contract, however, which, I was later told, restricts the loss of blood; so maybe the manner of my descent had been a blessing in disguise. The Laguna, meanwhile, had smashed to a halt in similar circumstances, running off the road into the very same bog. The driver tried vainly to clamber free but he was pinned to his seat by the buckled windscreen across his legs, no longer rigid glass but millions of individual fragments, loosely held together by laminate membrane. All around, people stopped their cars and ran to help. The driver tried to excuse his behaviour and told them that he hadn't seen the cyclist in time. But everyone else had seen the cyclist, at least before the crash. Where was he now?

Further up the road, Andrew had jumped on his brakes and brought his car to an emergency stop. Leaping from the driver's seat he ran back to where the collision had taken place and witnessed a scene of utter devastation. The crumpled bike lay in the middle of the road, missing a front wheel which was now some distance away. Its panniers had been destroyed and their contents of clothing, food and camping equipment were scattered over a wide area. The front of the Renault Laguna was caved in and the shattered windscreen was inside the car, across the two front seats. Its roof was extensively dented and sunroof smashed. All in all, the vehicle was a complete write off yet it had only collided with a pedal cycle. There was no trace of the cyclist; it was as if he had been wiped from the face of the earth.

## Out of the Blue

Another motorist in this line of cars was Simon, a former medic in the armed forces and one-time member of the elite S.A.S, also holidaying with his family on the Isle of Skye. Minutes earlier, Simon had been towards the back of the queue when he was overtaken by the Laguna. As a result, he was actually in a position to watch the collision right there in front of him and, like Andrew further ahead, had immediately realised a collision was inevitable. There was just not sufficient room for the manoeuvre which the driver of that car was attempting. Upon impact, Simon watched aghast as the cyclist flew like a rag doll perpendicular through the air, ten or maybe fifteen feet higher than the roof of the Laguna. Fortunately, he was also able to see where the body came down; in that flooded peat bog by the roadside.

With the entire line of traffic at a standstill, Simon ran to where I lay, submerged and motionless in the cold black water. He thought that it was too late; surely I was already dead. He leapt into the bog and its temperature took his own breath away. It was deeper than expected and he sank until only his upper body remained clear. Gently, Simon lifted up my head. There was no sign of life, movement or any reaction at all. Convinced he was dealing with a corpse, he nevertheless refused to give up hope yet and pushed his fingers into my mouth to ensure that the airway was clear. Only then did he hear a slight moaning, realising with relief that maybe, just maybe, there was a possibility that the life of this unfortunate cyclist could be saved.

Moments later he was joined by Andrew. An off-duty nurse had been in another car and she had seen Simon locate the cyclist. She now pointed towards him and encouraged the male drivers to go and help. Simon and Andrew were then joined by a third man named Paul, a school teacher who was also on holiday. Directly behind Simon, he too had been overtaken by the Laguna and watched in horror at the inevitability of it all. Andrew and Paul had no hesitation in leaping into the chest-high water to help. They knew that the cyclist would die if they didn't get him out of there soon. Yet as they began to move me Simon noticed the severity of the injury to my left leg. It appeared to be almost severed above the knee. Simon was worried that if they carried me too roughly my leg may become detached from the rest of my body. So he carefully held both parts of my leg together as Andrew and Paul dragged me out of the water and up the steep banking to the edge of the road. The professionalism and medical expertise of these men, together with two female nurses who had been in another car, was truly remarkable.

After my rucksack and jacket were cut away, Andrew made an assessment of my injuries. He saw that both of my hands were very seriously damaged, so extensive in fact that they would probably result in amputation. There were also numerous fractures to my left leg and a large section of flesh had been torn from my knee and thigh. Although very serious, those injuries, Andrew thought, were not life-threatening. His main concern was that he could feel numerous broken bones around my rib cage and spine, a punctured lung was already apparent and I may also have broken my neck. There remained a dangerous possibility of damage to my vital organs from those broken bones if there was any unnecessary movement. It was vital, therefore, that I was kept warm and absolutely still until an ambulance arrived. Simon kept a comprehensive first aid kit in his boot; those limited resources were all that they had to try and stem the heavy loss of blood.

Thirty minutes later, an ambulance came. Its crew felt that medical facilities on the Isle of Skye were inadequate for injuries of this severity and a helicopter air ambulance would be needed to fly me to the mainland.

This time, it took nearly two hours for the helicopter to arrive, by which time I had begun to drift in and out of consciousness. Somehow, I don't know how, I managed to tell Andrew that my name was David Watson. I also told him that I was married to Julie and even passed on her telephone number. The air ambulance was going to fly me to Raigmore Hospital at Inverness, on Scotland's east coast. Andrew wanted to accompany me there but the weight of an additional passenger prevented this from happening; it would have put the chopper beyond its safe flying limit.

In the meantime, the police and fire brigade had arrived from Portree, and my injuries were such that they decided to treat the collision as potentially fatal. The road was closed in order that the Laguna be recovered for examination and so that the scene might be photographed for the Accident Investigation Department. The driver of the Renault wasn't injured; he was arrested for dangerous driving and taken to Portree police station ahead of being formally interviewed.

Andrew, Simon and Paul were now covered in a mixture of my blood and the stinking black slime of the peat bog. There was only one thing to do. The fire brigade told the three of them to stand at the edge of the road while they were hosed down. They were soaked to the skin but at least the water was now clean. Andrew had rented a holiday cabin at a nearby hotel which had washing and drying facilities, so they went there to get cleaned up. Half an hour later they were stripped off and sat around in towels while their clothing was washed and dried, talking about what they had just seen. The collective opinion was that if David did survive, his hands and left leg would most likely have to be removed.

At the scene of the collision the police identified some significant marks on the road surface. These suggested I had tried to take evasive action. Just before impact, I'd turned to my left and onto the nearside verge. The actual impact had been on that verge and not on the carriageway. This showed that, for some reason, the car driver had actually turned to his right. Perhaps, when he knew that a crash was inevitable, he chose to hit the cyclist rather than the cars he was overtaking.

# 17

*

# Julie's Diary

WHAT happened next is best described by my wife, Julie. On the advice of staff in the intensive care ward at Raigmore Hospital, she kept a diary. Here is her account.

*Monday 11th August*
I arrived home around 2.30pm; earlier than usual, but it would give me chance to catch up on some paperwork and then take Toby for a walk on the moors, before taking Dan to work at 4pm. I hadn't been home long when the telephone rang, but the line was dead and I hung up. It then rang for a second time and a lady asked: 'Is that Julie?' I said I was and she told me she was ringing from the Isle of Skye. I panicked and asked: 'Is it Dave? Is Dave alright?' I began to feel anxious when she told me she was a police officer and that Dave had been knocked off his bike. I was trying to be calm because I knew Dan was upstairs, but every time I asked if Dave was okay she wouldn't commit herself. He would be flown to hospital by an air ambulance, but they didn't know

if it would be Glasgow or Inverness. I took her details and she told me they would call back when they knew which hospital Dave was to be taken to. My initial thoughts were that the police officer would call back saying Dave was going to be put in plaster and that I would have to drive to Scotland to bring him home.

Dan had been standing on the stairs while I was on the phone, so I told him what I knew. My mind was racing and full of questions. Should I set off now? What should I take? what about Dan? What about my work? What about Toby? What about Dan's work? Should I ring anyone? Dan was wonderful. He calmed me down, he was so grown up. I even imagined the journey all the way back from Scotland with Dave sat in the back of the car with two broken wrists and his leg in plaster. I really did think that it was just going to be more of an inconvenience really. I had no idea how badly injured he was, which was maybe a good thing.

I decided that the first person I should ring was Haydn, one of Dave's closest friends. In a crisis, when Dave wasn't there, he was always the next person to call; I knew he wouldn't mind. He answered with his usual 'hello, chuck', probably thinking I wanted a lightbulb changing or something trivial. But that wasn't the case and he could tell I was upset. He was at work but said he'd leave for our house straight away.

I had to try and sort out both Dan and our dog, Toby, and suggested that Dan should tell his work he couldn't come in tonight. There were so many calls to make I lost track, but then the police called back and said Dave was being taken to Inverness. Again the officer didn't give any details but she said he was at Raigmore Hospital, a place I had never heard of. Dan brought me a map and I hadn't realised just how far away Inverness is. The police thought Dave might still be transferred from Inverness to Glasgow at a later stage, but it was best to start making our way to the north of Scotland. Even at that stage I imagined Raigmore Hospital to be very small, so if he was to stay there then he couldn't be that badly injured. Little did I know that Raigmore hospital is a large trauma hospital which specialises in serious road traffic, outdoor pursuit and skiing accidents.

I called Dave's sister, Julie. Her husband Tim was already in Stirling, as he was working in Scotland. The phone calls went on and on and I knew that I had to go to Dave and that Dan would be best at home. Hopefully I wouldn't be away too long. Dan made himself busy looking at flights for me on the internet and then a nurse from the A&E at Raigmore phoned. Dave had arrived and she described his injuries as a broken leg with damaged hands. If anything, though, her phonecall just got me more worried. It was what she wasn't saying rather than what she was saying, but I gave her my mobile number and she promised to call me straight away if he was to be transferred. I spent the next few minutes telling neighbours, making phone calls and packing clothes. I stood in the bedroom with an overnight bag. What should I take? Enough for one night? Maybe two? At one point I just stood staring at it.

Dave and I have travelled all over the world in our time together and seen many countries, including much of Europe, Scotland several times, Canada, New Zealand and Singapore, to name but a few. I have always planned ahead, made lists, packed Dave's, Dan's and my own clothes, sometimes packing weeks before. This was different. I packed a washbag, a change of clothes and a few other items. I did not realise then, but I hadn't packed a hairdryer, hairbrush, mobile phone charger or nightclothes.

Haydn arrived just before 4pm and we dashed straight off, hoping to be back in a couple of days at the most. As we left, Dan was standing in the kitchen being his usual calm self and acting very mature. I tried to make light of the situation as I didn't want him to panic at my leaving him alone and going so far away. As Haydn and I got into the car I confessed that I thought the situation was probably more serious than I first thought, but that I wanted to protect Dan. I think Haydn had already come to the same conclusion after I mentioned how Dave had been flown by air ambulance to Inverness from the Isle of Skye. He set the sat-nav for Glasgow, but I explained the change to Inverness and that it may change yet again as we set off to Scotland while awaiting further instructions from the hospital. We had only been on the road twenty minutes when a female doctor treating Dave confirmed that he would remain at Inverness. She gave us directions and an update on his condition; he was sat up in bed and chatting, she said. That was a great comfort to me as we continued our way north.

At the start of the journey the sat-nav told us we would arrive at Raigmore at midnight, which meant an eight-hour journey. In fact, though, the long journey passed quite quickly. We had one short break on the M74 for coffee and a few more phone calls. We talked about all sorts of things and Haydn must have felt awkward as, earlier in the year, he had made this very same drive to Scotland with Dave to walk the West Highland Way. Now, a few weeks later, he was driving his best friend's wife to his hospital bedside. Thanks to the quiet roads, we arrived at Raigmore Hospital at 11pm, an hour earlier than expected. I was surprised at the size of the hospital. It looked enormous.

After parking the car we went to the A&E department, where we were taken straight through to intensive care. I pressed the buzzer and a few minutes later a nurse appeared and told us that Dave was with the doctors, could we wait for a moment? I was upset as we sat in the corridor and then a nurse named Susan McPherson came and showed Haydn and I into a small room furnished with comfy chairs and a sofa and soft lighting. I imagined this was the kind of room where people are told bad news. She brought us a tray of tea and explained that the doctor would be along shortly.

Eventually, Mr Renshaw, the consultant, entered the room. He was wearing a green surgical gown and hat. We all introduced ourselves and he told us he was going to take my husband into theatre. He described Dave's injuries and said that Dave had been hit head-on by a car while cycling in Skye. The car, it seemed, had been overtaking another car and crashed straight into Dave. Haydn and I gasped. I had convinced myself that someone had maybe clipped his bike from behind or that he had turned into an oncoming vehicle, not been hit head-on, that just doesn't happen to pedal cyclists. Mr Renshaw, though, was a very calming influence. I remember him being very tall with huge hands. He told us that in another car had been a consultant anaesthetist who was on holiday, but he had stopped and rendered first aid to Dave at the roadside. Mr Renshaw was very complimentary about the treatment Dave had received due to this man, who he named as Andrew from London. He said that although Dave was being prepared for surgery I could see him for a short while. The surgery was to clean out Dave's wounds as there was a lot of grit, glass and stones which, if left in place, would cause infection. What I did not know was that Mr Renshaw had begun his working day at 8.30am. He had already worked many more hours than would be expected and yet here he was, about to commence multiple surgeries on Dave through the night.

We were then taken into the intensive care unit. As we entered, Susan asked if I had ever been into such a ward before, which I hadn't. She then told me that Dave would look different as there would be a lot of tubes and wires going into him and that I was not to worry about that. I felt as though I was prepared, so we walked into a large dark room barely lit by small side lights, with background noise from various machines beeping. I followed the nurse to a bed in its own mini ward that was also surrounded by machines. This bed was raised high and it was then that I saw Dave for the first time, with tubes protruding from just about every part of his body, leaning back on the pillows.

I had not been prepared for this. This wasn't Dave's face I was looking at but that of his late father, Jack, an image I will never forget. His head and face were swollen much bigger than normal, his eyes protruded and his cheek bones had disappeared completely. His neck was huge and so was the front of his chest. Most noticeable was a big swelling to the right side of his head. He did not look like the man I had kissed goodbye only three nights earlier.

My insides shook and my body twitched. I felt helpless seeing him this way. We couldn't stay long as the consultant was ready to operate but I asked if I could touch him. All I wanted to do was hold his hand, but I couldn't as both were bandaged to the elbow. The nurse said I could touch his upper left arm so I stroked it and gave him a kiss. I told him I was there but couldn't tell if he knew. His eyes were shut but, for a split-second, he opened them and gave me a quick and almost awkward cheesy grin. Haydn was at my side and convinced me that Dave was aware of my presence.

When the hospital staff took him to surgery, we were taken back to the family room and told the operation would take a couple of hours. In fact it took four, during which time Haydn tried to comfort me but all I could do was sit and wait, in between pacing the floor. I was trying so hard to stop my body from shaking but couldn't. And then, at 5.30am, Mr Renshaw came to see us. He had just finished in surgery and explained the extent of Dave's injuries. The left leg was badly broken and would need pinning, but the most serious problem was that a large piece of flesh around the knee was missing and would need a skin graft.

The surgeon then described the damage to Dave's left hand and said, again, there was flesh missing with tendon damage and dislocation of the thumb and fingers. He explained in great detail what kind of surgery Dave would need and I was trying to take it all in. He then touched his own right hand. I was expecting pretty much the same as his description of the left, but Mr Renshaw said that this injury was one of the worst he had ever seen. He described how the skin had been cut across the fingers on the palm of Dave's hand and torn all the way back to his wrist. He said there was tendon damage to all the fingers and that it would need surgery by an expert in hand injuries. A colleague of his had looked at the hands but was not happy taking on such a complicated operation, so they would locate such an expert and find out where he or she was working.

I was allowed to go and see Dave but they warned me that I should prepare myself for more tubes and machines, as he now had a ventilator helping him to breathe. Mr Renshaw explained how this was necessary because Dave's body had been through such trauma and it was just one thing less for the body to deal with. Haydn and I walked back into the ward. Dave was laid on a bed, his legs covered with a sheet, arms at his sides and wrapped to the elbows in plaster casts. As promised, tubes were everywhere and some were connected to machines at either side. The ventilator went straight into his mouth and nose and I could hear the air go inside his chest. As it did, the chest inflated, going first up and then down in a quick movement. I had never seen anyone on a ventilator and it was nothing like those seen on TV. The nurse gave me a chair and I sat alongside him. I couldn't take it all in. Dave looked so frail and needy, a way I had never seen him look before.

After his marathon shift of twenty-two hours, Mr Renshaw finally went off duty. His surgical team had worked through the night to stabilise Dave's injuries and prevent any infection. Haydn said he would go and have a rest in the family room, so that I could spend time alone with Dave. I lost track of time. My chair was to the left of the bed so that I was facing him and each time the ventilator passed air into his lungs I watched as his chest rose and fell in shuddering jerky movements. I was so close my chair shook with the vibration every time the ventilator pumped oxygen. At about 7.30am I heard the radio. It was the Terry Wogan show on BBC Radio 2 and I wondered how he could be laughing and joking when everything had changed for us. Dave should be in his tent now, somewhere on the Isle of Skye. But no, someone had caused him to be in this position and so many people were concerned about his well-being.

After a few hours Susan handed her responsibilities over to another nurse when her shift ended too. This new nurse suggested I get some rest. We were now in the morning of second day and I had been awake for over twenty-four hours so, reluctantly, I joined Haydn. He had managed to grab a couple of hours sleep but he still looked tired. He was going to try and sort out accommodation for us. That proved quite difficult as this was the middle of the holiday season. Everything seemed fully-booked but he finally managed to get us a twin room in a nearby hotel. The owners allowed us to check in at 9am as we hadn't had any sleep all night.

However, I just wanted to get back to the hospital and sit with Dave, although I knew he was in good hands and the staff were wonderful. After a shower and a change of clothes there followed endless phone calls and we went back to the hospital to meet my brother-in-law, Tim. He was clearly shocked when he saw Dave and stayed the rest of the day. Later, Dave was taken off the ventilator and was now able to breathe unaided. I felt helpless and out of control of the situation but just wanted to be with him. I kept talking to him, in fact I never stopped talking, but there was no response. I felt so tired, it was difficult to keep my eyes open but I needed to be there. He made the odd facial movement but little else.

After Tim had left, Haydn persuaded me to try and get some sleep in the hotel, but it turned out to be a bad night. We left the hospital quite late and when I finally got into bed I struggled to fall asleep. When I eventually did sleep I then woke up suddenly and was very tearful. I was sobbing out loud and just couldn't stop myself. I had already woken Haydn up and I knew that I would be disturbing the other hotel guests, but I was unable to stop crying. Haydn was really good. He comforted me and listened to my cries and I couldn't have got through that night without him.

I was so angry at the person who had done this to Dave, who had done it to us. I was hundreds of miles away from home having abandoned our son, and here in a hotel with just a few belongings. I was desperate to get back to my husband and wanted questions answered. Who was it that did this to him? Was it a he or a she? Where did he/she live? Were they with anyone else in the car and why did they overtake with such reckless urgency? My husband had worked so hard all his life and deserved to do the things he had always dreamed of, but now all of that might be over simply because someone wanted to get somewhere a couple of minutes faster. Was this person having a sleepless night like me? Did they understand just how ill and injured my husband was? I begged Haydn to call the police just to try and get some answers. I sobbed for hours.

I was awake and dressed before 7am and tried to eat some breakfast, but I had little appetite. I had to force down each mouthful and just wanted to be with Dave and for him to be well again. When we got to the hospital there was a positive sign. Though he was still under the constant care of the nurses, Dave was moved to a side room and though he had his eyes closed for most of the time, he would very occasionally wake up and give me a reassuring smile. When the nurses were turning or cleaning their patient I went outside to deal with the endless text messages and phone calls. There were so many that I couldn't reply to them all and, although people meant well, they left me feeling utterly drained.

Mr Renshaw, meanwhile, had obtained the name of a specialist hand surgeon in Leeds, a Mr Shaaban, who agreed to do the surgery whenever Dave could be transferred back to Yorkshire. I wanted to be with Dave for the journey but that would only be possible if it could be done in a fixed wing aircraft rather than a helicopter. Mr Renshaw assured me that he would try to make that happen.

Dave still had lots of tubes in his body and oxygen continued to be pumped into his nose. This was vital as on top of the punctured lung and chest problems he had also developed pneumonia. He was in terrible pain and very agitated, he even swore occasionally and said he was going home, complaining that he hated being in this situation. Every now and again Haydn and I had to point out his left leg, which was held together with a metal cage. He was struggling desperately at times, trying to lay on his side or on his front. Each time he tried to move and couldn't we tried to show him why. He would look at the leg but then, a second later, we would have to go through the same ritual.

As the hotel was now fully-booked, Haydn and I spent the next couple of nights in hospital accommodation which, although very basic, was sufficient for our needs. There was little change in Dave during this time, he was still very restless and Haydn or I were constantly with him.

Mr Renshaw, however, remained very concerned about Dave's hands. Secretly, he feared he would have little choice but to amputate Dave's right hand at the wrist, and he would probably have to amputate two of the fingers on the left hand as well. The prospect of such drastic surgery was very troubling to him and he knew he would need my consent to carry out such an operation, as I was next of kin.

On the Wednesday, Mr Renshaw informed me that he wanted to take Dave back into surgery. He explained what he was going to do - hopefully just a cleaning of wounds to avoid infection - and I was asked to sign consent forms but, in my psychological state, I didn't really grasp their full implication. Thankfully, when Mr Renshaw came to see us afterwards he told us everything had gone very well. I noticed him gently stroking Dave's right arm. He said they were very pleased with the right hand but that it had caused a slight panic during theatre when blood began to spurt out as the dressings were removed. They had started the operation without a tourniquet thinking there was no longer a blood supply to his hand. Yet although they were shocked at the sudden appearance of blood they were also delighted because that now meant the hand could be saved rather than amputated - a procedure I had earlier signed consent for without realising. Mr Renshaw explained how Dave's hand had been saved by his fitness, which ensured the blood flow was much better than expected.

Although that was very much a plus, the following day brought a less positive development. The patient, it was decided, remained far too ill to be transferred to Leeds and so would have to remain in Inverness until Monday. I was devastated. My main worry was Dan, who was at home by himself, but I knew I had to stay in Scotland with Dave.

With each new nurse I tried to explain that Dave could withstand any amount of pain, it was being out of control of his own decisions that he struggled to cope with, especially if he couldn't sleep on his side or front. Every time he tried to twist his body around, either Haydn or I had to pull him down onto his back. That felt so cruel but we were trying to protect his leg from further injury. We were in limbo. The healing process could not begin until the operations were over in Leeds and yet here he was in such agony.

By Thursday night I was beginning to feel ill due to lack of rest and, for the first time in four nights, I got a decent amount of sleep. I woke up early the next morning and went back to the ward, where the nurse said Dave had endured a restless and difficult night but was now sleeping. He had found a comfortable position, partly on his side, and looked just like a baby. He had needed this sleep so badly; I just sat by his side and watched him.

On Friday night, Dave was transferred from the ICU to the high dependency unit. Having decided that he was going home, Dave had tried to get out of bed and had to be retrained by the nurses. He had also pulled out his chest drain, which was removing the excess fluid from his punctured lung, although the staff assured me he had not harmed himself in the process. There were a few more positive changes in that the swelling to his head and chest was slowly receding and he was increasingly able to move about the bed more easily. He was still confused about his injuries though, and convinced that if I were to get him his clothes he would simply be able to go home. He began to say the oddest things, but that was the effect of such a massive shock to the head and the amount of morphine he had been prescribed.

The following day, Dave was again due to go for surgery so that his wounds could once more be cleaned out. I woke very early and in an attempt to let Haydn sleep a little longer sneaked out to the hospital. I chatted to Dave when he was awake and when he nodded off I wrote in my diary, which was fast becoming something of a routine. It was to be a very long and frustrating day. The surgery was scheduled for 1pm but we were still waiting at 7pm when they told us that it was to be postponed until Sunday, due to other emergency surgeries taking place. Haydn and I left Dave at about 9pm to go and get something to eat before bed.

By 7am I was back at Dave's bedside and relieved to see him sleeping peacefully. The nurses said that the previous night, though restless, had not been as bad as the others. It was the first time that Dave had been in a proper deep sleep so Haydn and I walked into Inverness. It is a beautiful city and I couldn't help thinking how much Dave would love it. We would have to return when he was well. Back at the hospital, it was mid-evening before they took him to surgery. I just had time to kiss him and tell him how much I loved him and then he was gone. We were told he would be there for three hours and then be back on the ward.

We spent the time having a meal in a nearby pub and then took another short walk into Inverness, but when I still had not heard from the hospital by 10.30pm I began to get upset. This was taking much longer than anticipated. At 11pm Haydn and I went back to the hospital, where we were told that Dave was still in surgery and invited to wait in his room. For ten minutes, we sat awkwardly on plastic chairs alongside an empty bed until a doctor came in to see us. He began talking but I could only see his lips moving and there was a buzzing sound in my head as panic began to take over my body. 'Is Dave alright?' I managed to ask. I wanted the doctor to say 'yes', but he didn't say that. 'David has been taken to recovery,' he replied. During surgery, Dave's heart-rate had increased considerably, meaning he would have to be monitored. A blood transfusion would also be necessary.

I had been told that as soon as Dave was out of recovery

and in HDU I would be allowed to see him, but instead we were left waiting in his empty side ward for two more hours. Again I began to feel more and more anxious by this further delay and grew worried that we were not being informed what was happening. At 1.35am the telephone rang on the reception desk outside. A nurse answered it and immediately shouted to a male colleague that he was needed urgently in recovery. There had been a cardiac arrest. The male nurse raced along the corridor towards the recovery room where Dave was having his blood transfusion.

I looked at Haydn, he had heard exactly the same as me. The hair stood up on the back of my neck and my body began to shake and go out of control. I stood up and could feel my legs pacing backwards and forwards, but I wasn't actually moving. Neither Haydn nor I spoke a word but I knew that he was sharing exactly the same thoughts. Panic swept through me. I was scared to know the truth but told Haydn to ask if it was Dave who had suffered the cardiac arrest. I was too frightened to go beyond the doorway.

Haydn tried to stop a nurse in the corridor and ask if it was David Watson to whom they were referring, but she dashed straight past without answering. Minutes later, Marie, the nurse who had been looking after Dave, came and reassured us that it was not Dave who had had the heart attack and things moved quickly after that. Dave was taken onto the ward and soon we were allowed to see him. He was wearing an oxygen mask but responded when I touched his arm and the nurse said he was doing fine. He was on drugs to reduce his heart-rate and clearly very tired but I knew that he was in the best of care. We left him at 3am.

On Monday morning when I arrived to see Dave he was awake and gave me a wonderful smile as I approached his bed. He said that he was pleased to see me and didn't want me to leave but I had no intention of going anywhere. He was looking better than at any time since the accident and I was relieved to hear him talk. His voice had changed and what he said made sense, so he was getting back to normal. Haydn joined us mid-morning and he too was overjoyed to see and hear the person we knew after such a worrying time. The fact that Dave now seemed to be out of danger persuaded Haydn - who had been so selfless and done so much - that he could finally begin the long drive home. We said our goodbyes and I will be forever grateful for his friendship. Without Haydn's help and support I could never have made it through the past traumatic week and I was aware it had placed a tremendous burden on him. I said I would call later with an update on our proposed flight to Leeds.

The rest of the day I spent chatting with Dave. We spoke about his holiday, his accident, his injuries and what would happen next. I tried to fill in all the missing pieces of his last seven days. I fed him his lunch and evening meal; it was lovely to see him eating again. And I stayed at the hospital until 9pm, relieved that we could hold normal conversations after a week of confusion, upset and anxiety. That evening I went back to the hotel room and followed the usual routine of phone calls before collapsing into bed at midnight; it was to be the first night I could sleep virtually free from anxiety.

And then the day dawned when we flew back to Leeds. I fed Dave his breakfast and gave him a wash and a shave; tasks I would continue to perform for many weeks to come. As was now becoming the norm, the scheduled time to leave came and went but still we waited until, at 3.30pm, Dave was finally strapped to a stretcher, wheeled to an ambulance and off we went to the airport, where a small yellow light aircraft with only a pilot, co-pilot and paramedic awaited. Within five minutes we were heading down the runway and, before too much longer, Dave was sound asleep. Just over two hours later, we were in Leeds General Infirmary.

# 18

\*

# The Darkest Hours

MY own memories of that week in Inverness are vague. I had no idea where I was or how I had arrived there. I was in a different place, drifting through space. At times I could see myself laid on a hospital bed but couldn't feel it beneath me. I wasn't dead. Death would surely be peaceful and tranquil, not filled with terrible pain. I drifted in and out of agony.

At least I could take comfort from how, when I began to wake up more regularly after the first couple of days, Julie and Haydn seemed always to be at my bedside, albeit with a concerned look on their otherwise familiar and friendly faces. Physically, I was in great pain. Every little movement to try and alleviate the discomfort was a major battle. Both my hands and forearms were heavily bandaged and I was unable to move them. My left leg had a huge open wound above the knee; it looked like a piece of raw liver that had just been chewed by a pack of dogs. From ankle to thigh, it was encased in a metal framework to keep the jagged ends of the broken bones apart, so that it could be set correctly at a later date; a major reconstruction with the help of titanium plates and screws. And there were my other injuries too, of course: the broken ribs, broken vertebrae and the punctured lung from which I had developed pneumonia.

Reading Julie's diary later was fascinating, as it revealed plenty of detail that my badly swollen head had failed to register at the time. Some of the nonsense I spouted was astonishing. One day, I told Julie to 'get the speed boat serviced because we are going to need it', yet we don't even own a boat and never have. On another occasion, when asked by one of the doctors, I was unable to name the current Prime Minister. I said it was John Smith, who had once been leader of the Labour Party but who had died some twenty years earlier. My mind was clearly in complete turmoil.

Previously, I had never so much as considered taking my own life but, back then, I thought that death would come as a welcome release. I could find no respite from the constant pain, no comfort or decent sleep. There was no night and no day. The low lighting of the intensive care unit was always the same, without any noticeable change. The sedatives and high doses of morphine I had been prescribed worsened my mental health. In one of my more lucid moments, some five days after my admittance, I recall asking Haydn if he knew how I had received my injuries. He told me that I had been in a crash on my bike; hit by an oncoming car. Remarkably, I could still picture that road as it passed through open moorland. I asked Haydn what sort of car it had been and he told me, a Renault Laguna. 'Well, that wasn't a very fair fight, was it?' I said. 'No, lad. It wasn't,' he replied.

During my career as a road traffic policeman I had dealt with many similar incidents resulting in death or serious injury, so I knew that given the speed at the point of impact, an accident such as mine would usually result in the death of the cyclist. The more I thought about it, the more I grew convinced that I had cheated the grave. Sometimes, the realisation that I'd beaten such odds actually induced a state of euphoria. And, despite the pain, I was blissfully unaware of the serious extent of my injuries, or the length of time they would need to heal. Julie and Haydn knew, but I did not, though whether this was a result of the morphine rendering me incapable of understanding or because the doctors felt that I had enough to cope with, I am not sure. Either way, some of my injuries would stay with me for life.

I was also vaguely aware that we were now into the second week in August and that I had booked to go trekking and white water rafting in Nepal with Dan in eight weeks' time. I knew that I had a broken leg but my ignorance was such that I thought it would take only six weeks to heal. I assumed that my hands would just need the lacerations stitching up and then my fingers and thumbs would work. Doing the mental calculations I concluded that I would be ready to leave for Nepal in October. I didn't want to miss that opportunity. I had waited years to visit the Himalayas.

THE next six weeks were a combination of high dependency wards, single bed side wards and, as I continued to recover, general wards. I also had three more major operations, numerous X-rays and physiotherapy. The nursing staff were often too few in number and therefore unable to look after the patients in their care adequately. Julie became my chief nurse and carer, almost as a full-time occupation. She grew proficient in giving me bed baths, shaving my face and brushing my teeth. She fed me almost all of my meals other than breakfast and was at my bedside every day for hours at a time. She changed the bedsheets, brought me pyjamas and made me high-calorie food, whatever catered for my needs.

## Out of the Blue

After one of my operations I regained consciousness and found that I had been returned to the high dependency unit. This was divided up to accommodate individual beds with glass partitions between each. I became aware of an intense and unbearable heat. The nurse explained that I was covered with something called a huggy sheet, a sort of plastic quilt cover with a machine attached that continuously pumped hot air through a hose. It was almost impossible to cope with but I was assured that the heat would increase my blood circulation and therefore speed up the healing process. The huggy had to be in place for twenty-four hours and I was unable to sleep throughout the entire period.

Never have hours and minutes passed so slowly. There was a clock on the wall but whenever I looked at it the hands wouldn't move. The intense heat got even more difficult to deal with than the pain; I was so hot that beads of perspiration formed little rivulets all over my body. I was on a saline drip to replace the fluid but it poured out quicker than it could be replaced. All I could think about was getting through those twenty-four hours and then I would be able to rest, but I was wrong. When the huggy was eventually removed I was again moved into a side ward where, psychologically, I felt I had reached my lowest point.

To make matters worse, during one of the operations my left hand had been sewn into my groin, a surgical procedure known as a pedicle flap. This was the method by which skin, flesh and blood vessels were transferred from my groin to my left hand, replacing the flesh that had been torn away during the crash. The pedicle flap needed to remain in place for a minimum of three weeks before a further operation could be carried out to separate my hand from the groin. Throughout that time I was unable to move my left hand or arm at all. I was also unable to use my right hand, due to the serious injuries and the fact that it was encased in a huge splint and dressings. My legs fared little better. I'd had a major operation and skin graft on the left leg, which was now immobilised with a splint from ankle to groin, while the full length of my right leg was now also bandaged as it had been used for spare parts to repair my other injuries. An operation had been carried out to remove nerve tissue from the calf muscle of this leg, which was then used in the reconstruction of my right hand. The skin on my right thigh had then been peeled off and used to provide the skin graft on my left knee and thigh.

Not surprisingly, I felt completely helpless. All four limbs were immobilised and my head was the only part of my body that I could move, luckily enough given my broken vertebrae. I was in a side ward and unable even to press the emergency buzzer to summon assistance. If I needed help from the nursing staff during the night I had to wait until a nurse happened to walk past and then try to attract her attention by calling out to the corridor. The broken ribs and punctured lung meant that just trying speaking in a raised voice was painful, so that was a real challenge too. It was during one of those nights that I asked a nurse to telephone Julie. That night, I needed my wife to be with me and she didn't let me down.

My mind was in a dark, frightened place, somewhere I had never before visited and I felt desperate and vulnerable. My body was broken and for a while my spirit was too. Julie came back to the hospital and sat with me through the night, listening while I talked. Just having her there made such a difference. I already had an idea of the daily struggle which Julie endured in order to spend those hours with me but she never hesitated to come straight back when I needed her.

My confinement reminded me of an autobiography I had once read by Brian Keenan, the former hostage in Beirut. The part I identified with was when he described how he and the other hostages would be moved from one building to another. After making them stand in the middle of the floor watched over by heavily armed guards, their captors, starting at the ankles, would wrap packing tape around and around their legs and up over their entire body until the hostages were covered completely, apart from the nostrils through which they breathed. These living 'mummies' were then loaded into a coffin-like metal box welded to the underside of a truck and driven to a different part of the city. Although I had not read Keenan's book for quite a while, it was a haunting image that had stayed with me. Now, I felt, I knew at least a little of what he had endured.

Mercifully, however, the darkest days did pass and in time I began to adapt to my situation. I realised that I could not struggle against it anymore because my arms and legs simply did not work. For the first time in my life, I became submissive. It was clear that only the passage of time could heal my wounds; I had to learn to be patient and allow that process to take its course. And, sure enough, within a couple of weeks my wounds did begin to heal and my mental stubbornness began to return too. No longer was I prepared to accept broken promises by doctors and consultants. Instead, I wanted answers. When would my stitches be taken out? When would I have the pedicle flap separation to free my left hand? When would the splint and wires that had been drilled through the broken bones of my fingers be removed? And if those procedures did not take place when the doctor said they would, I would call them to account, often as they made their rounds the following morning. I have no doubt that the doctors became thoroughly fed up about this; I noticed that they would take a step back or hurry past my bed while speaking to their junior colleagues. But if I couldn't hear or understand what they had said about my treatment I would simply call them back.

Towards the end of my stay in hospital they could doubtless predict my questions before I even asked them. Can I get up and walk? Can I have the catheter removed? Why am I still taking so many drugs and medication? Can I go home today? And if not, why not? In short, I was regaining control over my life and self-confidence.


ON my ward there were three beds down each side of the room - six in total - and most of their occupants changed every two or three days. Myself, I was parked here for about four weeks and during that time lots of other patients came and went. Some were great characters and good company. Others were nothing but a nuisance, but it didn't take long to realise that a higher level of tolerance has to be developed to allow for people being in fear or great pain.

In a bed at the opposite corner of the ward was Malcolm, a real toff who spoke with a plumb in his mouth. Malcolm was a retired army Major and he spoke to everyone as if they were inferior. Certainly, he was not the sort of bloke I would have expected to find in the NHS; he'd have been far more at home in the finest of private hospitals. He also made it clear that he didn't want to socialise with us other patients and was isolated by having the curtains drawn constantly around his bed. He kept himself to himself.

Nor had Malcolm learned the art of tolerance towards the rest of the inmates and nursing staff; he continuously complained about anything and everything. If a mobile phone rang he could be heard to shout 'Oh God, not again' from behind his iron curtain. If the phone was answered he would again start moaning, declaring in a loud voice that it was against hospital rules to use mobile phones on wards. He complained if other patients' visitors stayed too long or spoke too loudly, and he was rude and insulting to the nursing assistants if his lunch happened to be late or the wrong meal arrived.

One evening, at about 9pm, the ward was unusually quiet. All the visitors had left early and from behind the curtain I heard Malcolm shout: 'Whoever has got that TV on will you please turn it off?' More of an order than a request. Tragically, for him, the television in question was my own. Most of the other patients used earphones so that their neighbours were not disturbed, but I was unable to pick them up so, for me, it wasn't possible. Anyway, I chose to ignore him until, using his walking stick to move his curtain to one side, he looked directly my way and told me again, in no uncertain terms, to use the headphones.

'Bollocks,' I replied.

'What did you say?' he huffed.

'I said bollocks. I can't use the headphones because I can't pick them up. You're nowt but a miserable old bugger. It's only nine o'clock. Why don't you stop moaning for a change and let everybody have a bit of bloody peace?' The curtain was discretely dropped back and no more was heard from Major Malcolm.

In the bed opposite the old grump was John, an equally ancient Glaswegian with a rich Scottish accent. Sometimes, though, John's quiet raspy brogue was barely audible due to his treatment for throat cancer. Ten minutes after my dispute with Malcolm, John began to get dressed and I assumed that he was going outside for one of his regular cigarette breaks. As he walked past the bottom of my bed he nodded to me in acknowledgement.

'Hi John, are you going outside for a smoke,' I asked.

'No, not yet,' he replied, with a wide grin on his face. 'I'm going home to collect me fecking bagpipes. It's just too fecking quiet in this fecking place for me.' And with that he nodded over towards Malcolm in the corner.

In another bed was Tony. He didn't have any visible illness or injury but, the following day, was due to have a biopsy for a suspected cancerous growth. Tony liked to talk to other patients and went out of his way to make friends. He was obviously worried about his operation and must have been mulling things over in his mind when he started telling me about his philosophy on life.

'It's like this, Dave,' he said. 'You go through life and everything is running along smoothly. I'm happily married, just retired, house is paid for, got a few bob in the bank. The kids are grown up and in steady relationships and grandchildren are on the way. Life seems too good to be true, but then it happens. The big fella upstairs just leans down from the heavens and smacks you right in the face with a big custard pie.' I was chuckling at this amusing philosophy on life when Tony added: 'And that was your custard pie moment, Dave. When you were cycling on the Isle of Skye.' Despite the pain of my broken ribs, the thought of that tickled me greatly.

During my stay in hospital I was overwhelmed by the number of people who turned up at my bedside. Some had travelled many miles. Some I had lost touch with years ago and some were not in good health themselves. I felt very humbled that so many friends and relatives went to such trouble to give me their best wishes. My sister Julie and her husband Tim were regulars. Julie and I spent hours playing dominoes just to pass the time and when it was Tim's turn he would usually smuggle in some fish and chips.

At my lowest ebb, I desperately wanted the operation to remove the pedicle flap and release my hand from my groin. Perhaps then I wouldn't feel quite so helpless. But there would have been serious risk involved for that process to take place; it could mean me losing part of that hand. At that time, it was a risk I was prepared to take because I felt so trapped and helpless but, fortunately, this was also the time that friends Mark and Debbie came to visit me. They both spoke to me with compassion and understanding, making me realise that I had to put up with short-term pain and discomfort for the longer-term benefits. That was a turning point in my recovery. I now knew that I could and would endure the discomfort that had been getting me down.

Another regular visitor was my daughter, Hayley, who faced something of a dilemma. A couple of weeks before I was to leave hospital, Hayley was due to go on a round-the-world trip with two other girls. Everything was booked and they had an itinerary that would take them to the USA, Fiji, New Zealand and Australia, before returning home in a year's time via Malaysia and Thailand. I know that she felt terribly guilty about leaving me there in hospital but I insisted that she should go and could see no reason for her to miss out on the opportunity of a lifetime. Hayley was fulfilling one of my own ambitions and I would be able to share it with her via regular emails and through the photographs that she posted on her internet blog.

# 19

\*

# Release from Captivity

IT was six weeks since I last saw myself in the mirror, but even from my hospital bed I could tell that I was losing weight rapidly. Over two stone had vanished already and I weighed less now than I had at any time in my adult life. The most noticeable change was to my upper arms. Before the accident they were muscular and well-defined. But now all shape had disappeared and the flesh hung down like an old woman's 'bingo wings'. My forearms had shrunk too, to the extent that I now had wrinkled flaps where previously there was muscle. I was little more than skin and bone.

No doubt my legs were in a similar state but the splint on my left leg and the dressing on my right prevented me from seeing those. Still, at least my catheter had been removed and I was finally able to visit a proper toilet again, albeit in a wheelchair. There was a mirror in there, fitted to the wall. I looked into it but the face that stared back was someone I barely recognised. My hair had grown considerably and was now longer than it had been in thirty years. My face was sunken and gaunt, and my eyes bulged prominent.

My doctors were worried by this weight loss and a dietician was asked to monitor my progress. Julie continued to try and make me eat plenty of high-calorie food, but it made little difference. I had completely lost my appetite and felt as though I was being force fed. I also suffered sleep deprivation and dreaded night time coming around. It felt as if I was the only person on the ward awake and it was rare that I'd sleep for more than a couple of hours. The nights were endless and when I eventually did fall asleep through sheer exhaustion, I would inevitably be awoken by one of the nurses wanting to take my blood pressure or give me some form of injection.

Surely, by now, I should be starting to feel better - but instead my health seemed intent on deteriorating. So far I had been free of any infection, but I became convinced that the longer I remained in hospital the more likely it was that I would be struck down by one of those deadly superbugs. I no longer required daily medication and felt sure that if I was to be discharged Julie could look after me just as well at home. Happily, some seven weeks after my admission, the medical staff finally agreed, although whether that was because of my progress or the fact that they were fed up of me pestering them every day I couldn't say. Either way, the time had come to go.

And what a homecoming it was. Ninety minutes after leaving hospital in an ambulance I was being carried into our home in Cross Hills, near Keighley. Julie and Dan had been busy; there was now a bed for me downstairs, together with a bedside cabinet, lamp and anything else that might make me more comfortable. Toby, our border terrier, was also thrilled to see me and couldn't contain his excitement as he jumped all over me trying to lick my face.

For Julie, though, that evening was the start of a new and demanding routine. Firstly, she would wheel me into the downstairs bathroom. Then she had to lift me up and prop me against the wall. She would then undress me and wash me all over, while I stood naked on my right leg and rested the splints covering my hands on the washbasin. After which it was time to dress me in pyjamas and dressing gown, before I was lowered back into the wheelchair so that she could give me a shave and brush my teeth. This first night home also gave me the chance to see the top half of my body for the first time in almost two months and, again, it came as a complete shock. It would be no exaggeration to say that I looked like an inmate of a World War Two prison camp. My body was completely emaciated and it was possible to count each and every one of my ribs individually. The pectoral muscles in my chest had disappeared, to be replaced by two small folds of skin hanging down from my scrawny chest.

Even so, being back at home was wonderful. Julie lifted me out of the wheelchair and we sat side by side on the couch in our living room. Dan was upstairs in his room and Toby was curled up in front of the fire. Heavenly. The TV was switched on but we weren't watching it; the volume was turned down as we chatted. We had both been through times when we feared we would never share such simple pleasures again and agreed that our relationship now was stronger than ever. We spoke of the positive things that had come out of a situation which could have ended tragically. We also spoke of the change in Dan. Suddenly, he seemed so grown up and was now prepared to take on responsibility and put other people first.

We talked about of our love for one another and how we must never take that love for granted. And we reflected upon the help and support received from so many relatives and friends. I told Julie that this had been a very humbling experience for me and that one day I hoped I would get the opportunity to thank those people properly.

I MAY have been home but there was still a long, long way to go before my rehabilitation was complete. The splints and dressings on my hands and metal splint on my leg ensured that I would still be entirely dependent on Julie for quite some time to come. She had already been off work for two months; caring for me at home kept her away for a further two. I was full of admiration for how she dealt with being a full-time carer. I don't know how I would have coped if the roles had been reversed.

Life soon settled into a pattern of restrictive and boring confinement indoors, a thing I was not particularly used to. But it did give me time for reflection. I wrestled with the concept of whether good or bad luck had been significant in the outcome of my accident. Maybe it was a combination of the two. Since my arrival at Inverness hospital, I had repeatedly been told how lucky I was. Medical professionals had been present at the scene of the accident. Simon had seen my body land in the peat bog. It was lucky that I had been so fit...and so on.

Yet it was difficult to recognise this good luck when I was in such enormous discomfort in hospital, unable to move my limbs and dependent on other people for my every need. And, anyway, what about the bad luck? What if I had cycled to Stornoway rather than Skye? Or if I had left the Sligachan Hotel ten minutes earlier with the other cyclist and been a few hundred yards further along the road?

Ultimately, the more I thought about it the more I came to the conclusion that luck is an irrelevance; and that life is just a matter of pure chance - neither good, nor bad. After all, if I hadn't been fit then I wouldn't have been on that type of holiday to begin with, would I? No, this was all just a freak accident and a rare one at that.

But maybe my friend Debbie had been correct when she first visited me in hospital. Julie and I had told her how the accident occurred. We told her what we had gleaned from people at the scene and my doctors. Debbie listened with interest and then summed everything up in a single thought: 'You were just meant to be here, it's not your turn to go yet.' Debbie has spent her whole career employed by the NHS as a radiologist and I consider her to be a wise and intelligent woman. She has her own religious beliefs and is aware that I lack the same conviction, but her rather simplistic answer does prevent an awful lot of soul searching.

During the first two weeks at home I tried to occupy myself by filling in the blank spaces between the few known facts of the accident. I made a couple of telephone calls to the police on the Isle of Skye and I found them very helpful, but they had very little in the way factual evidence. They told me the name of the car driver and said that following his arrest he had been interviewed and stated that, for some reason, he just hadn't seen me. He was a local and knew that road well. Although he admitted his mistake he could not offer any other explanation. He had been charged with dangerous driving and would later attend court.

Julie asked me to phone Andrew, the off-duty consultant anaesthetist who looked after me at the scene. We had his telephone number but knew very little of what had taken place prior to speaking with him; it turned out to be quite an emotional call. He picked up the phone and I asked: 'Is that Andrew?' 'Yes,' he replied and I told him: 'You probably don't know me, but my name is David Watson.' Before I could go on he yelled back: 'I do know you, I certainly do know you. How wonderful to hear from you both. I cannot believe that I am speaking to you.' He was clearly elated. We were using the speaker phone facility, which meant that Julie could join in the conversation too.

Andrew then went into detail about what had happened, much of which we had not heard before. His modesty was such that, when it came to describing his own involvement, he deliberately understated the part he had played in saving my life. He recalled the incident with such clarity that Julie was crying throughout the call. We could never adequately thank this man for what he had done for me on that day.

Andrew's only regret, he said, was that the weight limit of the air ambulance had prevented him accompanying me to the hospital, one hundred miles away. Again this would have caused him and his family tremendous inconvenience as it would have taken him to Inverness when his car and family were on the Isle of Skye, but that had been his last consideration. Some months later I received correspondence from a solicitor that was quite enlightening, confirming my earlier assumption that Andrew was a man of incredible modesty. Andrew had carried out neurological tests on me at the scene of the accident. He checked for eye movement, verbal response and, finally, motor response, assessing me as being at Scale 3 on a system called the Glasgow Coma Scale, used to determine levels of consciousness. The lowest point, or starting point on this scale is level 3 and it goes up to a maximum of level 15, which is considered to be normal.

I checked the significance of level 3 and was shocked to discover that it is only used in the most severe of cases, that is, when death has already occurred or, alternatively, when the casualty is in a deep coma. It was really only then, many months after leaving hospital, that I realised just how close I had come to losing my life. I suspect that Andrew's modesty will prevent me from ever finding out exactly what he did to help me that day, but I do know that I will always be indebted to him.

# 20

*

# Back to Reality

I RETURNED to hospital as an outpatient at least twice a week and they were long and tiring days because the journey had to be made by ambulance. In Leeds there was a specialised hand physiotherapy department that hospitals closer to home didn't have. The physios were limited as to how much they could do while other treatment was ongoing but they did teach me some 'passive physio' on the fingers deemed sufficiently healed. I was to repeat these exercises every day at home.

As usual, though, I took things to the extreme, spending many hours trying to get some movement back. As a result, almost every night the pain in my hands would wake me up. My fingers were bent into a position resembling claws rather than human hands, they had been in splints for so long that this was the position they naturally adopted. The only way to relieve the pain was to do more physio, which is what had caused the pain in the first place. It was a vicious circle and caused me many sleepless nights.

One luxury I had been deprived of for many months was

a hot bath. I pondered this and decided that if I temporarily removed the leg splint and climbed the stairs on my bum, using my right leg for leverage, I could reach the bathroom. I persuaded Julie that this would be possible and she agreed to help me. I struggled up the stairs and then once I was in the bathroom she got me undressed and sat me in the wheelchair, so that she could push it towards the bath. The plan was that I would then slide out and into the hot foamy bubbles.

It was all going perfectly. Julie held onto the wheelchair, I lifted up my legs and dipped my feet into the water. Then I pushed against the back of the chair which allowed my legs to slide forward. I was almost there but, just before my backside slid over the edge of the bath, disaster struck. I'd forgotten about my testicles. They were hanging down between my legs and caught on the edge of the bath as I was sliding across it. I let out a scream but they were trapped with all my body weight pressing down on them. My hands were still in the splints so I was unable to relieve the situation by taking any weight on my hands. In my panic I pushed myself forward with my elbows, splashed down into the water somewhat gracelessly and laid there feeling sorry for myself and swearing under my breath.

It was only then that Julie noticed blood in the water. In my desperation to relieve the pressure on my gonads I had banged my left knee on the bath taps and, in doing so, had suffered a circular cut on my skin graft where the skin was newly formed. The wound was bleeding profusely and I wasn't sure just how the new skin would heal. I would be much more careful about how I got into the bath in future.

About six weeks after my return I had an appointment with Mr Templeton, the consultant whose brilliant carpentry skills had put my left leg back together. The X-rays showed that the broken bones were now fixed and that new bone had started to grow around the plate and numerous screws which were to remain in place. It was a tremendous relief when he removed the metal leg splint and promptly threw it straight into the rubbish bin. He told me that I could now learn to walk again and that the leg was capable of bearing my full weight. He would also arrange physiotherapy sessions with his specialist team, who deal purely with leg and foot problems.

Although it had been a bad break with a number of separate fractures, it now looked as if my leg was going to make a good recovery which lifted my spirits considerably. For a number of weeks previously, I had believed that the leg was strong enough to bear some weight and, in Julie's absence, I would often try standing on it or walking short distances around the house. Now, thanks to the doctor, I could walk on the leg without incurring the wrath of my good lady.

I was introduced to Sam McGregor, the physiotherapist who was given the task of restoring the limb to full health. My first impression wasn't very favourable. He was very young and probably inexperienced, but I couldn't have been more wrong. This young man was perfect for me in that he pushed me to my limit and sometimes beyond. There were times when I came out feeling physically sick with the effort and pain I had been put through but the results were remarkable. Sam monitored the degree of flex I had in the knee and, week after week, it was a story of continuous improvement. He also worked hard at building up strength in the leg and I found it perversely satisfying at the end of some sessions to see that he was almost as out of breath as I was due to the effort he put in. Sam was the perfect tonic for me and again my spirits were lifted by the improvement in my ability to walk. My hands, though, remained less keen to progress, despite the best efforts of my hand physio.

## Out of the Blue

It was during this period that I began to notice how some casual acquaintances would make incorrect assumptions and comments about my situation. I lost count of the times people told me I would be 'all right' when the car driver's insurance company paid out my compensation. Obviously, the people who made such comments had never suffered any serious and lasting injuries themselves. Usually, I would ask the person how much money they would want for selling me their own right hand. A non-committal answer would often follow, so I offered them a million pounds. 'No,' was the inevitable answer. And if I upped my offer to ten million, the answer stayed the same. I was making the point that no amount of cash could adequately compensate me for either the loss or restricted use of my hands.

Deep down I knew that unless there was a good return in their functionality, my dreams of how I wanted to live my life in future would be shattered. I grew ever more confident that, given time, I would get back the majority of strength and mobility in my left leg. But the rate of recovery in my hands continued to be pitifully slow, for reasons which I had perhaps chosen to ignore. The earliest clue I ought to have picked up on came from the hand surgeon himself, Mr Shaaban, back in the recovery room. After having just carried out lengthy and intricate reconstructions, he showed me some photos that he had taken before the operation. Both hands were photographed and each one looked absolutely horrendous. They appeared as if they had been placed on a butcher's block, with the palms facing upwards, and then someone had attacked them with a meat cleaver. My hands were swollen to such an extent that they were huge, a fact so far been hidden from me by thick bandages and splints. The cuts appeared to be so deep that if it wasn't for the swelling they would have gone right through, from one side to the other.

I don't know why Mr Shaaban showed me these photos and I cannot remember if he even asked if I wanted to see them, but after I had stared hard for a minute or so I said: 'They are awful, the worst injuries I've ever seen.' His reply took me by surprise. 'Yes,' he said. 'They are the worst injuries I've ever seen too.' I suppose I should have heard alarm bells ringing at that comment, but I had such faith in his expertise that I let it go by.

Then, about three months later, we had a further consultation and this time Julie asked with Mr Shaaban a direct question: 'Will Dave ever regain full use of his right hand?' The doctor replied that while there would be some improvement he couldn't say how much, and that it would never be as useful as it once was. That was something of a blow. At that time the only functionality I had in the hand was in the little finger, the rest was completely useless.

Julie by now had decided that she should ask the questions I perhaps didn't want to know the answers to, so the following week she spoke to Kelly Harrison, a senior physiotherapist, who was also dealing with my case. Julie asked Kelly if she had ever treated anyone with hand injuries as severe as mine. I could tell that the question made Kelly feel uncomfortable but Julie persisted and urged her to give an honest answer. When it came it wasn't really what we wanted to hear.

The bottom line was that I had finally begun to realise that my life would have to change forever. Without the full use of my hands I was not going to live the life envisaged when I retired from the police force. I was determined, however, to remain as positive as I could and have tried to stay so ever since. One day, for example, I intended (and still do intend) to cycle again, even if that meant moving both brakes and gear levers to the left side of the handlebars, where I might be able to exert a little more control. I also hoped to go hill walking and non-technical mountaineering. However, I knew it would be unlikely that I would ever participate in rock or ice climbing again, or tackle anything sufficiently dangerous that it would require me to handle a climbing rope.

Another depressing consideration was that my skills and knowledge in the building trade were no longer going to be of much use. Prior to the accident, home improvement projects had become a way of life; it didn't matter whether it was a new kitchen, bathroom, replacement windows or the building of a garage or conservatory, I always found time for such projects on days off from the police. There was also the maintenance of my three renovated houses to think about, which would now be virtually impossible for me to carry out. Simple everyday problems like replacing a leaking toilet cistern or bleeding a radiator would have to be done by someone else. For the first time in my life I was about to start paying other tradesmen to do jobs that I would once have gobbled up with ease. Knowing that I had the knowledge, equipment and time to carry out these tasks was a constant frustration, as was having to rely on other people.

I had no intention of retiring from the world of work entirely, however. Fortunately, before the accident, I had attended a training course designed to provide its students with the qualifications needed to submit Home Information Packs, a legal requirement at the time in the world of housing and estate agency. If I was to continue down that path, my weekly hours of work would be entirely at my own discretion, as I would be employed on a part-time, self-employed basis. Even now, I had one eye on taking time off for holidays and travelling. The cold hard reality, though, was that I would be unable to accomplish any of these things without a dramatic improvement in the condition of my hands.

Another shock to the system was the perception that people increasingly had of me; that I was now disabled. I had appointed a solicitor to act on my behalf in dealing with the car driver's insurance company. He urged me to submit a claim for the Disability Living Allowance, but I could not yet think of myself in that way.

This was followed by a telephone call to a former tutor at Craven College. I told her about the accident in Scotland and what injuries I had suffered. I also told her that I wanted to resume the part-time 'A' level course that I had begun last year. About a week later I again spoke to this tutor and she informed me she had conducted a meeting with a college department dealing with students who have 'special needs'.

A QUESTION I am frequently asked is whether I feel any anger towards the driver who caused my injuries. The short answer is no, I do not.

I have experienced frustration that my injuries are not healing as quickly as I expected them to or would have liked. I have felt frustration at my lack of independence. But anger? No, not really. However, I do know that at times of stress and worry, my wife Julie has felt enormous enmity towards this man. She has been furious about what he did to me personally and us as a family. Others have said that they too, in the same circumstances, would share that anger. So why am I so different?

Well, I can only put it down to my personality. It isn't that I am not capable of feeling and showing rage because I am, but I tend not to dwell on past events. In fact, I don't really look too far into the future either, rarely beyond my next holiday. I live very much in the here and now and accept that, while this accident could so easily have been avoided, there was no deliberate intent to cause me injury.

In short, it was an accident. It really is as simple as that. I'd like to think that the man responsible became a better driver because of it. I am also conscious of the fact that it is probably he who will have the nightmares rather than me. I don't remember anything of the accident, my brain has simply blanked it out. But the bloke who hit me will never forget when the cyclist he 'didn't see' came crashing, head first, through his windscreen. That moment will live with him forever, certainly longer than any punishment a court might impose.

During my telephone conversations with the police on the Isle of Skye they kept me up to date with the preliminary hearings at court, and a date of 4th December 2008 was fixed for the trial. In the meantime I heard from my solicitor that the driver had admitted liability to the insurance company, meaning he was likely to do so in the criminal court too. I arranged with the police that I would contact them afterwards to be informed of the penalty handed down. Julie wanted to drive all the way to Skye so that she could attend the trial and tell the court how this man had devastated our lives, but I could see little point in doing so. I persuaded her that it would be futile to even consider it. And yet as that date came and went I found I had no interest whatsoever in learning of the outcome. It was completely irrelevant to me. Nothing could turn back the clock.

# 21

\*

# Climate Change

IT is Friday 28th August 2009 and I have almost finished writing this book. Today may well have been a watershed in my life.

It began at about 9am when my friend Ian came to pick me up in his van, ready for a day's walking in the Lake District. In the back went the dogs, Ian's border collie Eddy and my border terrier Toby, who snuggled down for a couple of hours kip before we reached our destination. The weather forecast was mixed. Patches of heavy showers were anticipated and the temperature was somewhat cooler than might be expected at this time of year. Far from ideal then, but Ian works away from home and didn't have any other days available. Anyway, we weren't going to be put off by the odd shower.

Seventy miles later, Ian pulled into a lay-by on the A66, near to the White Horse pub. The dogs were released from their enforced captivity and were excited and eager to be off. But first we had to cross the busy main road, seldom the easiest of tasks and all the trickier on a Bank Holiday weekend. This might well be the most dangerous part of the day.

Once safely across, we then embarked upon a short stroll before turning off onto a track that stretched way up into the moorland hillside, heading for the summit of Blencathra. The sheer bulk of the mountain had been clearly visible from several miles away as we approached it from the east and today the summit was shrouded in mist, but the dark grey rocky arête of Sharp Edge stood out clearly against the leaden skies. That precipice would be our intended route to the top. Though the sight of Blencathra was a formidable one, the start of our walk, a gently sloping grassy path around the mountain to Scales Tarn, could not have been easier. The real mountaineering starts beyond the tarn. From there, we were to take the usual route up and across the imposing Sharp Edge before following a path to the summit and descending back down into the valley via Halls Fell Ridge. A circular walk of about six or seven miles, it encompasses two of the most spectacular ridge walks or scrambles that England has to offer.

I had attempted this very route with Ian and the dogs in December 2007 but, back then, it had been under wintry conditions and there had been a build-up of snow and ice on Sharp Edge. We had already completed Striding Edge and the summit of Helvellyn that very same day, so we arrived at Scales Tarn on the approach to Blencathra quite late on. While wandering up the path towards the tarn we spoke to some walkers coming in the opposite direction. They had bad news: Sharp Edge was effectively closed. Apparently, a climber traversing the arête had either slipped or fallen off the crest, before tumbling down its northern side, and was thought to be seriously hurt. The mountain rescue helicopter had been called in and they were evacuating the casualty as we waited. Given the circumstances, we decided to change our plans and take a safer route to the top. There is little doubt that this decision was correct. It later transpired that the unfortunate man had died from his injuries.

But now, just less than two years on, we were ready for another go. For Ian, it would be his first ascent of both Sharp Edge and Hall's Fell Ridge. For me, it would be my first return to the mountains since my cycling disaster around twelve months before. From leaving the van, it took us about an hour to reach the tarn, the traditional place for a lunch stop before the steep climb up to Sharp Edge. And no sooner had we stopped than the heavens opened. Swiftly, we threw our waterproofs on as the rain began to pour like a tropical storm, only without the warmth and humidity. In no time at all we were soaked, with nowhere to shelter from the gusty accompanying wind. The dogs were looking pretty sorry for themselves too, heads bowed and backs turned into the storm. They didn't even have the luxury of waterproofs.

Eddy cheered up a bit when I gave him a pork pie; well at least he did for a couple of seconds, which is about the amount of time it took him to swallow it, in one piece! Toby tried to show Eddy some doggy etiquette. He gently took his pie from my hand before dropping it onto the grass and then carefully nibbled at the crust to break it up into small pieces. Eddy watched intently, his own growler now somewhere deep within his stomach. When Eddy thought no one was looking he darted across towards Toby's pie, obviously intending to help him finish it off. Only a well-timed jab in the ribs from my right knee prevented him from swallowing Toby's grub as well as his own.

Meanwhile, back in the human world, the wind and rain had started to make my hands feel very cold; one symptom of poor blood circulation following half a dozen operations. I tried in vain to put my gloves on but it was hopeless. Then, as now, I had very little dexterity in the fingers of my right hand and am unable to bend some of them. Many have little or no feeling which adds to the problem. I couldn't tell if I was pushing my digits into the right finger holes or the wrong ones. Ian tried his best to help and for the next couple of minutes we both wrestled with the gloves but they were still only partly on. At least my hands were now covered and protected, but only about half the length of each finger was where it was supposed to be. It was the best we could manage and was going to have to do.

There was no point in standing around. Heavy rain and blustery wind don't encourage delay, so off we went up the footpath towards the start of the ridge. Unusually, there was no sign of any other climbers or walkers, the first time I had ever come across that sort of solitude on this particular mountain and I had been up it around ten times. Maybe it had something to do with the weather.

As we trudged up the path, the wind began to increase in strength. Time and again I was blown sideways, before managing to regain my balance and carry on in an upward direction. Ian was starting to have doubts. 'Are you sure this is a good idea,' he asked, doubtless thinking about the tragic incident of the time before. 'No, it's probably not a good idea at all,' I replied. 'But if it was easy then everyone would be doing it wouldn't they?'

We struggled on past a cairn that marks the start of the arête and the real challenge now was there to see. It brought to mind the writer Alfred Wainwright's description of this route: 'The crest itself is sharp enough for shaving and can be traversed only *à cheval* [shuffling along the ridge on your backside with legs astride] at some risk of damage to one's tender parts.' It was far too windy to even consider striding out across the top, that would merely invite the inevitability of being blown straight off the mountain. Our new route would have to be along the north face of the arête, taking a narrow and indistinct path about fifty feet below the ridge itself. This would still be very difficult; covered as it is with numerous large wet slabs and steep slippery rocks.

In the guide books, Sharp Edge is considered a 'Grade 1 Scramble'; yet in such conditions it was likely to be at least as difficult as a 'Grade 2', i.e. more difficult still. For the uninitiated, a scramble is best defined as something between a mountain footpath and a rock climb, in other words it may well be necessary to find suitable hand and footholds but, in normal weather conditions, ropes or climbing equipment are seldom needed.

Anyway, Ian and I set off along this undefined path, but the dogs were struggling. Usually they love a day out and had both experienced similar terrain before, but not in this weather. The track was tough to follow, often disappearing completely, and their paws skidded as they attempted to find their way across the steep sloping slabs. Normally, they have little trouble on steep ground providing they can get some grip, but claws are ineffective on wet rock and they were both far from happy. Several times, Eddy tried to turn around and go back down the ridge; maybe his sense of self-preservation was stronger than ours. Toby didn't show such open rebellion but there were moments when he skulked low to the ground and began whining. 'Stop crying,' I admonished him. 'You're supposed to be a terrier not a poodle. Terriers are supposed to be tough.'

The whole scenario was fast turning into something of an epic. Ian's doubts began to resurface. He complained that his boots were hopeless and he couldn't get any grip, as the sheer drop behind us grew increasingly threatening as we ascended higher and higher. My own fingers were little use in many of the holds, especially those on my right hand. By now I could at least partially bend the fingers on my left, although they remained considerably weaker than they had been before their encounter with the Renault Laguna. Also, I began to struggle with the lack of flex and bend in my left knee. I could manage to step up about twelve inches on that leg but, if the next foothold required a step greater than that, I had to switch feet and step up using only the right. There were times when I had to rely purely on balance and pray that my feet didn't slip from their carefully selected foot placements or I would be off, sliding down hundreds of feet of rocky and unforgiving mountain. It was too late to turn back now, though, so on we went, sometimes gently coaxing the two dogs, occasionally shouting or even bullying them, and often having to resort to physically lifting or pushing them forwards and upwards.

Now, the western end of this ridge abuts against the bulk of the mountain at a very steep angle. In order to gain that buttress we would first have to scramble up a sheer gully, which proved especially difficult for Eddy. Some parts were extremely steep and there was nothing but smooth rock to try to get a grip of. It wasn't too bad for Toby - I could simply pick him up and push him ahead of me - but Eddy was too big and heavy. Still he kept trying to go back down, so I had to stand behind him, forcibly turn him round and push him ahead while Ian encouraged him from above.

Eventually, after scrambling up the gully, we clambered out onto the exposed face of the buttress and there we felt the full blast of the wind. We hadn't known it earlier but on the northern side of the ridge we had been sheltered. Not any longer. Again, we scrambled up the slippery rock face for a couple of hundred feet until, finally, mercifully, reaching the gently sloping footpath that leads directly to the summit. At last, we were safe. Although the wind was at gale force, the path was quite wide and there was little danger of being blown away.

As seen from below, the summit was above cloud level

so, with very little visibility, there was no reason to dawdle. Immediately, we set off back down onto Halls Fell Ridge. Less challenging than Sharp Edge, this ridge is nevertheless considerably longer and itself has numerous sloping rock slabs that have to be crossed. On dry days these slabs present no problem whatsoever, it is simple to walk straight across them. Today was not one of those days.

On one occasion the blustery wind got the better of me and I lost my balance, falling onto my backside. And initially the slope was so steep that I was unable to halt my slide until, after travelling a number yards downhill, I suddenly came to an extremely painful stop. My left heel had snagged against a knob of rock, bending my knee back a couple of inches more than at any time since my accident. Gingerly, I hobbled to my feet and tried walking a few paces on some nearby vegetation, gradually increasing my weight on the leg. To my relief it felt okay. No lasting damage but it had been a close call. I would have to be even more careful.

And yet after only five more minutes on Fell Ridge the weather deteriorated again. This time we were delivered hailstones - in August! The wind again increased in strength and was now as strong as any I had experienced in these Lake District mountains. The dogs must have wondered what was going on as they crept forward, head down and eyebrows scrunched, against the particles of ice battering into them. At one point, Toby had gone about twenty feet in front until, noticing that I wasn't there, he turned around and lay behind a small boulder, body and chin flattened to the ground, in wait. He was trying to keep out of the wind and hail in the only way he could.

Yet still we pushed on and some three hours after we had started out, we found ourselves, wet, windblown and weary, back down in the valley, facing a pleasant thirty-minute walk back to Ian's van. My left leg ached and I was soaked to the skin but there was no mistaking the feeling. I felt exhilarated. This had been my return to the mountains and I had loved every minute of it. I had taken a chance, which was probably unfair on Ian and very unfair on our brave and loyal dogs, but we had faced some quite extreme conditions and come through them without any serious mishap.

Yes, I had pushed myself hard - probably too hard - and I knew I would pay the price for my pig-headedness during the forthcoming days, when I was struggling to get out of bed and barely able to walk. But it was not even one year ago to the day that I had been laid in a Leeds hospital bed, with my shattered left leg having just been rebuilt and the protective metal framework still attached. My hands had both been reconstructed and bandaged to the elbow. My broken ribs, fractured vertebrae and punctured lung were continuing to cause me immense discomfort. And it was then that I had asked the consultants, surgeons and physios charged with putting me back together how long they thought that would take.

'At least two years,' they had predicted, as one.

I do love a challenge. What's next?

# Epilogue

*

SO, was my cycling holiday worth it? Don't be daft, of
course it wasn't. If I'd had a crystal ball and could have
foreseen what was going to happen when I threw my bike in
the back of the car that evening, then obviously I would
have put down the keys, rung up the travel agent and
booked a Caribbean cruise for my wife Julie and I instead.

The fact is that I have been left with a broken body and
parts of it are beyond repair. And the surgery continues.
There have been ten operations to date and the hand
reconstruction is not yet complete. There have been times
when I just wanted the next year to be behind me. But then,
conversely, thinking like that is a waste of one's valuable life,
especially when you have been reminded just how short a
life can be.

No doubt I have lost forever the pleasures of winter
mountaineering and rock climbing. No longer can I hold a
squash or tennis racket. Something as simple as putting on a
pair of socks can be extraordinarily difficult, fastening shoe
laces or buttons is damn near impossible. But I am learning

to adapt and make the best of what I have. To swallow my pride and ask for help when I need it.

The impact on Julie's life has been almost as traumatic. She is now my carer as well as my wife. I accepted the risks involved in my chosen lifestyle, I always have and couldn't live any other way, but it is different for her. She has to pick up the pieces yet hadn't been a party to the decision-making process. When I first returned home from hospital, it often felt as if I was under house arrest. Some days the walls seemed to be closing in, but even this confinement was to have its positive side. It gave me the time to start writing my police memoirs and, once begun, they seemed never to end. In fact, so numerous were they that I haven't even been able to include them all here. All I had to do was remember a time, a place or a person and the memories came flooding back.

But there was another reason why I felt the need to write about what had happened to me. I wanted to create a written record of the accident that has now changed the life of myself and those around me. Late one night I was sat typing at the computer while Julie and Dan were asleep in bed. After a while I got bored of typing and, for the first time, began to read the diary that Julie had kept of that first week in Inverness. Reading Julie's account of that time was such an emotional experience that I was moved to tears. It made me realise that her life had also been devastated and that she had been through more mental torture than I could possibly comprehend.

I have often wondered if the driver who hit me has been on the same emotional journey. I now know that he was late for a meeting; with every vehicle he overtook saving him a few vital seconds. There had been little sympathy for him at the scene. My rescuers and some of the witnesses openly expressed their anger towards him. They had all driven patiently in the tailback of traffic, he had not shared their patience.

But, for now, who knows what the future may hold, certainly not me. Baring my soul in this way has without doubt been the cathartic experience that I was seeking. At least I'm still here and undertaking the journey myself.

Like me, the travelling dream is very much alive. I hope to resume the cycling holiday on the Isle of Skye before too long. I often think back to my final night on the Isle of Harris, laid in my tent and considering the possibilities of cycling through Ireland or Scandinavia, maybe crossing the Baltic. Or perhaps it would be overland trips through Africa or the Himalayas. I haven't given up on these adventures but, at the moment, I have to accept, reluctantly, that they are temporarily postponed. But who knows? With fortune going my way and if my life turns out to be interesting enough, one day I may continue the story.

# If you enjoyed this, you'll love these from Scratching Shed Publishing Ltd...

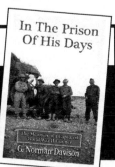

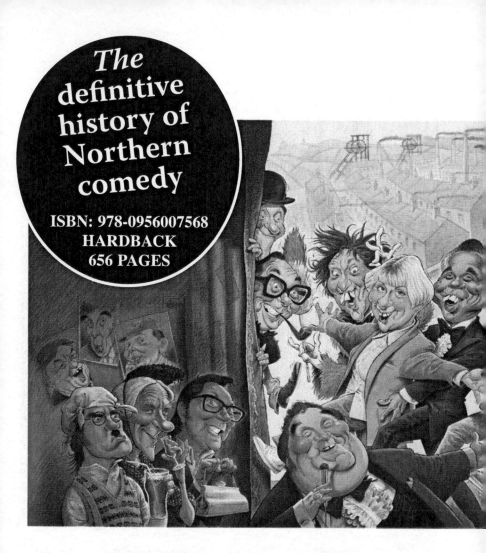

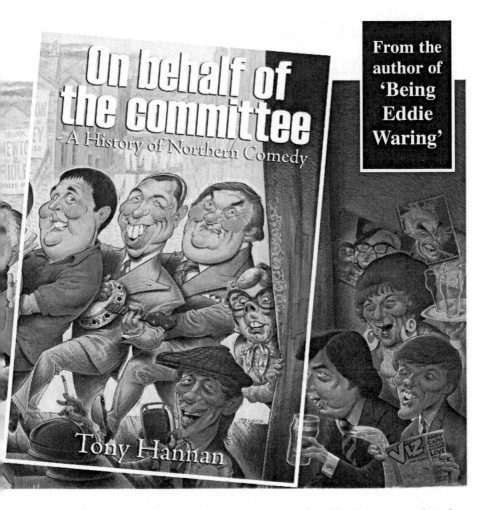

From the Industrial Revolution to our own comfortable 21st century digital
age - via music hall, Variety, working mens clubs, radio, cinema &
television - Northern-born comedians have consistently been at the heart of
popular British comedy culture, tickling the funny bone of the entire nation.

This witty and informative book questions why that should be so, all
the while charting an entertaining course through the careers of George
Formby, Tommy Handley, Gracie Fields, Frank Randle, Al Read, Jimmy
James, Hylda Baker, Jimmy Clitheroe, Les Dawson, Morecambe & Wise,
Bernard Manning, Alan Bennett, Monty Python, Victoria Wood, Ken Dodd,
Chubby Brown, The Young Ones, Vic and Bob, Steve Coogan, Caroline
Aherne, the League of Gentlemen, Johnny Vegas, Peter Kay and many
many others. Along the way, it also wonders why such a huge contribution
to the British entertainment industry should be so often under-appreciated.

Mostly, however, it is a rich celebration of British comedy history &
confirmation that you really do have to laugh - or else you'd cry...

# COMING AUGUST 2010
from Scratching Shed
Publishing Ltd...

# YORKSHIRE FOOTBALL
# - A HISTORY
## *Cameron Fleming*

ISBN: 978-0956252654

Scratching Shed Publishing Ltd